ENGLISH LANGUAGE, ENGLISH LITERATURE

ENGLISH LANGUAGE, ENGLISH LITERATURE

The Creation of an
Academic Discipline

Jo McMurtry

ARCHON BOOKS
1985

The paper in this book meets the guidelines
for permanence and durability of the
Committee on Production Guidelines for Book Longevity
of the Council on Library Resources.

Library of Congress Cataloging in Publication Data

McMurtry, Jo, 1937–
    English language, English literature.

Bibliography: p.
    Includes index.
        1. English philology—Study and teaching (Higher)—
History.   2. Morley, Henry, 1822–1894.   3. Child,
Francis James, 1825–1896.   4. Masson, David, 1822–
1907.   5. Skeat, Walter W. (Walter William), 1835–
1912.   6. College teachers—Great Britain—
Biography.   7. College teachers—United States—
Biography.   I. Title.
PE1065.M373   1985   420'.7'11   84-20534
ISBN 0-208-02060-8

To my mother, Evelyn Walker Ballard,
whose sense of the past as a treasured resource
has brightened the lives of her children,
this book is lovingly dedicated.

Contents

Illustrations

(pages 85–100)

Acknowledgments

I am indebted in numerous ways to the University of Richmond, without whose support this book could not have been written. A sabbatical leave in the fall of 1983 was only the most visible of these gifts. Dr. William Woolcott, chairman of the Faculty Research Committee, and the members of this group made financial help possible on numerous occasions. Dr. W. D. Taylor, chairman of the Department of English, contributed not only scholarly understanding of the problems of combining teaching with writing but practical help with regard to class scheduling. Finally, Provost Zeddie Bowen and Dean Sheldon Wettack approved my participation in a grant program that brought a microcomputer into my life, lessened by many times the mechanical frustrations of putting ideas into presentable form, and incidentally provided an ironic contrast with the pen-wielding labors of the Victorian professors this book is about.

Librarians on both sides of the Atlantic have been consistently courteous, knowledgeable, and interested. I have met with more than able assistance in the collections of the University of Richmond, Harvard University, the British Museum, the London Library, University College London, Cambridge University, and the University of Edinburgh. I have special thanks for the staff of the Mary Evans Picture Library.

James Thorpe III of the Shoe String Press made a number of suggestions about the manuscript for which I am most grateful, as I am for the ideas contributed by the anonymous reader of the first draft. These last were of particular help in the revision of the first chapter.

Finally, I would like to express my thanks to Herbert Rudlin and the staff of Adams Camera Shop in Richmond for the attention they gave to those of the illustrations that came under their care.

Introduction

Oddly enough, in view of the gray and solemn authority of the stereotypical English professor, the study of English language and literature as a respectable academic discipline is a fairly recent development, dating in the case of most institutions of higher learning only from, say, the 1860s. The newness of the discipline might perhaps have something to do with the tendency of its practitioners to take on an air of timeless profundity. We respect antiquity and tend to adopt it as a defense mechanism. If English literature goes back for centuries, five centuries at least in recognizable form, and even longer when threaded through the Middle Ages to be attached to the Anglo-Saxon language and thence back to the hypothetical realms of Indo-European, then a similar air of venerability might be seen to cling to the systematic study of these phenomena. This stratagem may have worked. Certainly the English Department looms like a monolith on many a college campus, for better or for worse, and to picture academic life without it requires an energetic bound of the historical imagination.

In taking our sights back to the 1860s for a sense of the general acceptance of this new discipline, we find a discrepancy between English and American academic contexts which, on the American side, simplifies the process. English studies were new to the typical American campus, but so was everything else. In America, the latter half—and particularly the latter quarter—of the nineteenth century included several waves of prosperity both economic and intellectual, and the founding of new institutions of higher learning (along with the revitalizing of existing ones) became a frequent endeavor. Thus an English Department could be installed without major dislocations. On the more traditional side of the Atlantic, among the gothic cloisters, adding an English Department usually meant rearranging and changing whatever was already there, with consequent objections and disagreements which often had a bearing on the direction the new discipline was allowed to take.

1

It is not the aim of the present study to trace through every twist and turn the paths by which English studies found their way over this diversified terrain. Such a comprehensive and complete work would not only fill many volumes but would, I suspect, transmit its message inefficiently to the audience with whom I hope to connect. This audience is both narrow and wide, depending upon one's perspective, for I hope to interest those who are drawn to the discipline of English either through sheer affection unclouded by practical concerns or a mixture of this affection with the grittier necessity of earning a living with it, that is, of teaching it. I am not setting up an exclusive salon. Everyone is welcome here, mathematicians, gardeners, guitarists. I am, however, realistic about the types of people likely to be fascinated by old examination questions.

In one sense, then, the audience to which I address myself is a narrow one. Yet within the general bounds of English studies, the possibilities for increasingly distant and complex specializations seem to multiply while we watch; in this sense my audience is a very wide one. And this diversity among English practitioners today, a diversity among ourselves and from our academic ancestors, is the reason for this book's concerning itself with flesh and blood, with four individual people and what they did, rather than with columns of figures stating how many students enrolled in what courses, in what institutions, during what years. I wish to emphasize a sense of common ground. And this common ground often requires more explanation than a recital of numerical facts would allow.

The fact is that for most of us, getting back to the Victorian age is a strenuous and sometimes startling mental journey. So much has changed. Things we take for granted—dependable library catalogues, for example—were not at all a part of the scholarly picture. Even the mechanical differences—gaslight instead of electricity, the slow advent of the typewriter, no photocopying machines let alone computers, pens which had to be dipped in ink once or twice a line—are easy to overlook, at least in their effect on scholarly endeavors. When Queen Victoria died in 1901, and the whole world joined with the British Empire in the feeling that an era had passed, the public looked back to the beginning of the Queen's reign in 1837 and marveled at the changes that had come about in the interim. Railways, telegraphs, universal education, new concepts of human rights—life seemed to have altered with dizzying speed. Could the erstwhile Victorians have looked into the following century from their vantage point of 1901, the dizzy sensation would have been unlikely to go away.

This study, then, will pay some attention to what Victorian life was like. In focusing on four scholar/teachers and their respective contributions to the emerging discipline of English language and literature, I hope to show something of the contexts in which they made their decisions, envisioned their goals, and succeeded to a greater or lesser degree in reaching them.

In some ways these four professors are a great deal alike—sturdy gentlemen, several of them in body as well as in mind, respectable, inspiring high esteem in their colleagues and their students. They lived in pleasant houses, filled with books; married affectionate and supportive wives; produced among them a total of eighteen children, many of whom became remarkable persons in their own right. Considering the statistics of the time, each of the four had a long life, attaining an average age of seventy-six years or a median of seventy-five, as one prefers. The four have differences as well as similarities, and these differences allow us to cover a lot of ground in our panorama of the nineteenth-century academic landscape. Henry Morley introduces us to University College, the most revolutionary educational experiment of its time and in the 1830s the first degree-granting British institution to establish a chair in English language and literature. Francis Child takes us to nineteenth-century Harvard, where higher education was rapidly evolving toward its present American form. With David Masson we find ourselves in Scotland, where scholastic excellence and experimental vigor were cherished traditions and where firm foundations for the study of English already existed. Finally, it was with Walter William Skeat that the study of English language and literature at last became an official, recognized academic pursuit at Cambridge University, where, as at Oxford, the innovation had been regarded with suspicion.

To shift for a moment back to the similarities of our four gentlemen, we find that each performed to a greater or lesser extent a rise in the social scale, a levitation due in part to intelligence and energy and in part to luck. Both in Britain and the United States the economy rose during the century; the United States found itself with a continent full of resources to exploit, and Britain perfected its techniques of exploiting other people's. In their rather undramatic way, education and scholarship received the benefits of commercial and imperial bounty.

Opportunities arose; horizons widened. Masson and Child became highly respected professorial persons, although each had been born into the working class, while Morley and Skeat, of middle-class origins to begin with, achieved prominence by shifting ground within this general category. Since the study of English is sometimes advertised as an aid to self-improvement, the careers of these four practitioners might be seen as a demonstration of upward mobility. Perhaps it would be more accurate to say that the society as a whole, having become increasingly flexible in the nineteenth century, was able in these cases to recognize and reward merit.

A further similarity shared by these four scholars forms something of an ironic pattern. Each in his own way was a popularizer. The riches of English literature presented themselves as a treasure trove to be brought into the light of public awareness—accurately, systematically, but with all possible celerity. Thus Morley left his history of English literature unfinished while he hurried from one lecture hall to another, addressing audiences of all types and academic levels. Child, sitting down to work in snippets of spare time, achieved a lasting monument in his ballad collection but found it expedient to bring out a less comprehensive and less authoritative edition some years before his masterwork appeared, so that as he continued collecting ballads, people would know what he was talking about. Masson's numerous periodical essays on literary subjects enlightened the general educated populace and thus helped prepare the way for more specialized studies in English, but as the essays were not written for specialists, they have not been recently reprinted and are for the most part unknown to the readership they helped to form. Finally, while Skeat's name has lived through many of his editions of medieval texts, others—scholarly siblings—have been superseded as knowledge has advanced in the philological and etymological fields which Skeat so industriously opened up.

This ironic state of affairs is perhaps my main motive for writing this book. Working as efficiently as circumstances would allow, these men were among those who dug the foundations for the academic discipline of English as we know it today. It is in the nature of foundations to be built upon, and thus to be obscured and taken for granted; but the occupants of the edifice today, still in its process of change, with a new wing here and a skylight there, may find their labors enhanced by an awareness of what came before. To this awareness I hope will be added some sense of appreciation. Our academic forebears were attracted to their work by a love of the English language and its literature, and this is still the case today, whatever changes our lives and our professions have undergone. In our secret hearts we feel we are very lucky people. And although the work of our predecessors may differ from the way we ourselves might have done it, they did it for us, and in thinking about them and their world, we are communicating with a part of ourselves.

1
The New Subject

To the present-day American or Englishman, objections to the study of one's native language and literature may be hard to imagine. We are so used to doing it. Perhaps we are equally used to being told to do it—or, if we are members of the English profession, to telling others to.

One could reel off a list. Practical reasons—one must speak and write correctly in order to get ahead in a competitive society—mix easily with patriotic and aesthetic ones. This literature is our own, after all; we should survey our own domain if only through pride of possession; furthermore, life in today's mechanized world requires some glimpses of a lasting kind of beauty, some connections with the past and with the ideals of the humanities. Through these exhortations runs as well a note reminiscent of the Protestant work ethic whose influence on our culture we are accustomed to seeing pointed out. The very act of reading the serious literature of the English language, whether that of past centuries or the quite sufficiently complex productions of our own time, is hard work, and therefore good for us.

Many of these ideas were familiar in the later half of the nineteenth century, where the present study is centered. They were, however, arranged in different proportions or attached to different objects. The idea of getting ahead in the world by using one's own language correctly might have puzzled many of those who made the decisions on what was or was not appropriate material for study; but the beginnings of this enterprise were present, for example, in the working-class education movement of the nineteenth century. With regard to the humanities, to the need for beauty and grace and a wider view of human potential, the role of literature was recognized quite definitely—but the literature was that of a different culture. For centuries Greece and Rome had provided the model, and the study of Greek and Roman literature was held a necessary illumination for a world otherwise barbaric. And finally, with regard to the beneficial effects of hard work, any proposal of studying English literature tended to lose ground at once, for a student would not even have to learn another language; the endeavor appeared not so much too difficult as too easy.

Should we wish a present-day analogy, we might notice some of the arguments raised today against the addition to college curricula of courses in film or television. Professorial hackles rise at once. Is academic credit to be given for an activity, and not at all a demanding activity, which the student might have undertaken on his own in any case? In which he need not even have learned to read? An activity which attracts to the classrooms of higher education those students of lesser ability who very likely could not survive the more demanding requirements of the traditional subjects? And, a crucial point in this line up of arguments, how are these students to be examined, on what standard of measurement are grades to be determined and credit hours disbursed? The analogy need not be labored point for point, and we may leave Media Studies to find its own way in its own time, but we do see here, curiously reflected as the scope of higher education continues to expand and diversify, some of the problems the new discipline of English will encounter in the nineteenth century.

Tributaries to the Stream: Wealth, Leisure, and Women

To say that the academic study of English literature is the direct result of the Industrial Revolution might be something of an oversimplification. The sources of English study are complex. (As, for that matter, of course, are those of the Industrial Revolution.) An awareness of the English language as a vehicle for literature can be seen early in the sixteenth century, when Wyatt and Surrey transferred their appreciation of the Italian lyric into their own language. In the same century, Henry VIII's dissolution of the monasteries scattered the contents of their libraries into private hands (the hands, not surprisingly, of Henry's supporters), and scholars then became curious about the manuscripts that came to light written in that forgotten language, Anglo-Saxon. Matthew Parker, for example, Archbishop of Canterbury and a pillar of the English Reformation, rescued manuscripts zealously and pro-

moted Anglo-Saxon studies as a means of emphasizing the independence of the Anglican Church.[1] And the treatment of English literature
as a historical continuum had its beginnings in the eighteenth century.

Nevertheless, it is the energy and resources of the emerging industrial age which created the social and academic context needed for
the systematic study of English. Money had a great deal to do with it.
By the nineteenth century, people had become richer; the middle
classes, including many who had risen to these levels with startling
speed, found themselves with more parlors, more bookcases, more
hours for social conversation and private pursuits. The family took in,
and arranged on tables in their library or in the parlors, the new periodicals—the monthly journals, say, filled with what we would call
"feature articles" on travel, on the latest archeological diggings in Egypt
or Cornwall, and, fairly often, on such bits of literary history as an
essay on the works of some little-known Jacobean playwright. This last
effort would include full descriptions of the plots, since no one would
be expected to have read the plays; and indeed the texts might well
exist only in some seventeenth-century quarto recently found in the
British Museum, with no modern reprints available at all. Thus, while
English literature was still ignored in the universities, while the sons
of this hypothetical family went up to Oxford or Cambridge (or Harvard
or Yale) to study Greek and Latin, the ground was prepared in middle-
class cultural life for an increasing appreciation of the native product.

With regard to the spread of new interests, the popularity of the public
lecture is worth noting. The lecture was the ideal outlet for middle-
class energy and earnestness. It was a social event, where one might
wear one's new clothes and meet one's friends, yet it was not frivolous—
quite the contrary. Self-improvement was an accepted goal among the
middle classes. This was in itself a new thing. The aristocracy would
not have thought of it, considering themselves to have been sufficiently
improved during the centuries in which their family identities had been
evolving; among the working classes, breaking away and "realizing one's
potential," as the phrase goes today, occurred fairly often as an individual achievement in the nineteenth century but was only minimally
built into the culture. And for those below the working class, the thousands of abysmally poor, more concentrated and thus more visible in
England than in America, whose main hope was to survive from one

day to the next and who are analogous today not so much to any segments of the developed nations as to the Third World, the idea of improving oneself in any way must have been difficult even to grasp, let alone to implement. But for the middle classes all things seemed to become dazzlingly possible. New systems, practical or aesthetic, scientific or literary, opened before them, and to sit in a lecture hall while some authoritative figure—part entertainer, part priest, or prophet— showed them a new perspective of the world had a strong appeal.

The lecturer on English literature fit in very well here. Some of what he said would be familiar, for many of the major works had always been read, more or less, though in a haphazard fashion. And the contents of the typical middle-class home library, English or American, could provide some help for the new idea of a systematic study of English literature. The lecture-goer might come home feeling inspired, look about his or her shelves, and make a start at once.

In such an inventory, the Bible and Shakespeare were basic and could be found in most home libraries, along with Bunyan's *Pilgrim's Progress*. Spenser's *Faerie Queene* retained its prestige, as did Milton's works, and Pope's; Thomson's *The Seasons* was a favorite. A few eighteenth-century novels might be admitted to the family's collection, but these were generally considered risqué, lacking in the modern sensivity to decorum, and they might be hidden from the unmarried daughters or at least locked in a glass-fronted bookcase. Nineteenth-century novels were naturally seen as the latest thing and were difficult for the purchasers to pigeonhole as to ultimate value, but Bulwer-Lytton, Thackeray, and Dickens would probably be represented. Of contemporary poets, Tennyson and Matthew Arnold would be welcomed, Browning was considered obscure, and Longfellow achieved success with *Hiawatha*. In the category of literature written in English, the family's holdings might end at this point, the other shelves being crowded with Greek and Latin texts (their purchase dating from Father's school days), works of history both ancient and modern, volumes of sermons, the sets of encyclopedias which were becoming an increasingly familiar part of the home scene, and bound issues of periodicals. The family simply saved these last as they came in and sent them off, once a year or so, to the bookbinder. The American home library formed a fairly identifiable subspecies, especially in its array of local periodicals. But the books in British and American homes tended to be much the same. English books were in fact highly favored by American publishers, as the existing copyright laws were too weak to cross the Atlantic and the latest Dickens novel, or whatever came to hand, could be printed up and sent off to the bookshops without any troublesome payments to the author.

Of the audience for the lectures, a large proportion was women. This is not surprising. Throughout much of the middle class, women were allowed the role of guardians of culture, in charge generally of the menfolk's rest and recreation with a dose of moral responsibility thrown in; women were supposed to point the way to Heaven. English literature fit in as an appropriate pursuit. As a hobby it was quiet, it required no expensive equipment, it had moral overtones (if one excised the eighteenth-century novel, that is; many men refused to let their wives read Fielding), and it was intellectually accessible in that it did not require learning an ancient language, or any language at all. The women attending the lectures, and doing a bit of reading on their own afterward, may have been aware of all these advantages and discovered a few more—the intellectual pleasures of perceiving causes and effects, perhaps, of drawing comparisons and making connections, of filling in an abstract outline with concrete examples, and above all, the delight of experiencing words well used. Women asked for more. Lectures led to reading lists, reading lists led to more lectures—to a sequence of lectures, often—and then, as a sequence of lectures has much in common with a course of instruction, to the idea of passing examinations and taking degrees. This overview is much simplified; the process was a complex one, and women invaded many fields besides English on their way to the cap and gown.

In this endeavor, two types of organizations particularly helped smooth the way. The "university extension" schemes begun in the 1870s had as their goal the bringing of university lecturers to audiences remote from the established halls of learning; in several cases, these efforts led eventually to the founding of institutions of higher learning to serve the populace which had been thus discovered. "Extension" audiences included women as a matter of course, since one did not have to matriculate in an existing institution in order to hear the lecture. The second type of organization specifically addressed the needs of women as the Ladies' Education Association.[2]

These last groups, functioning in the 1870s and 1880s under sev-

•

eral variations of names throughout both Britain and the United States, had as their object the preparation of women for admission to the degree examinations of major universities. They often served, in fact, as the thin end of the wedge in the process of naturalizing women in the universities, eventually to be admitted as regular undergraduates along with the men. By the end of the century, this goal had been achieved to the point that a woman undergraduate no longer appeared to the public to be a monstrosity. There were, however, intermediate steps and some curious gradations. (University College, London, went through a phase during which lectures for men met on the hour, and lectures for women on the half hour, to avoid the distraction of cross-gender mingling in the corridors.) With the passage of time, women were seen in a more realistic perspective; it was found that while some women might indeed fulfill the gloomiest visions of husband-hunting frivolity let loose in the halls of learning, others built on their opportunities and became educated human beings.

The effect of this incursion on the study of English was considerable. The universities' official publications—in particular the annual catalogues or calendars which often supply so remarkably close a focus on the academic life of the period—show again and again that the admission of women and a rise in the enrollment of English courses were simultaneous phenomena.[3] When in the 1880s and 1890s honors degrees in English were offered at several universities, women's names make up a substantial proportion of the lists of successful candidates; fifty percent and above is not unusual. (And, of course, some candidates have names of ambiguous gender, while others are listed by their initials.)

From the standpoint of the prestige of the new subject, its accessibility to women brought both good news and bad news. A certain amount of immediate prosperity was undeniable. The English professor increased in stature; from a rather tenuous position on the staff, from which he was liable to return to journalism, the pulpit, or other earlier haunts if his students' lecture fees dwindled, he found himself in demand, perhaps provided with an assistant, establishing something of an empire in fact. In the earlier phases of the new subject's growth, the feminine cast of its classrooms may have protected it from unduly jealous reactions from the more established disciplines. Women represented after all a new market. No large masses of students were being taken out of the traditional subjects to be shifted into this one.

But any field of endeavor—jobs, academic subjects, ways of life—which is associated with a lower-status group is itself going to be assigned a lower status. The very popularity of English thus became one of its problems. Discussions of the matter tended to center not on the question of women as such but on the question of the standards to be maintained; yet the danger of the new subject's vanishing into a sea of pink ruffles may well have affected the directions that were ultimately taken. Women did not advance to the podiums of the university classrooms whose seats they filled. They were encouraged to seek careers in the lower echelons of teaching, where opportunities were opening up quite briskly, and the woman who sought a graduate degree in English remained something of an anomaly into the early decades of the twentieth century.

In short, while women helped put English on the map by providing bodies to fill the classroom, they became an implicit liability when it came to demonstrating how hard the new subject was. Women as a sex were not considered capable of sustained mental efforts, even though an individual woman might eventually win some respect for her brain. The solution was a two-pronged one. English must be shown to be fiendishly difficult—especially at the upper levels where masculinity prevailed, but lower on the pyramid as well. And the rigorous standards would then reflect favorably upon any women students in the classes. If they could pass these exams, filled with publication dates, lists of authors, conjugations of Anglo-Saxon verbs, then they were clearly above the stereotype.

English studies were fortunate at this point, for the two aspects of the discipline, literary history and philology, which served particularly well as a source of impressive erudition, had a great many other benefits as well. Each was intrinsically interesting; each contributed to the sense of coherence which English studies needed. Although each had pre-nineteenth-century beginnings, there was still in the nineteenth century a spirit of discovery and systemization with regard to authors' chronologies or etymological roots. Students of English felt themselves challenged in this regard, rather than imposed upon.

Philology and the Antiquaries

Philology, the source of much of the new English professors' erudition, was not a new study in itself. The vocabulary and grammar of Latin and Greek had been grist to the scholarly mills for centuries. English simply had not ranked very high—a rather sloppy, miscellaneous language, it was thought, with inelegant pronoun declensions and mongrelized vocabulary. This attitude changed abruptly in the early nineteenth century with the arrival from Germany of what one might call a burst of philological illumination.

"From Germany" is an oversimplification, even though the most influential scholars were based in German universities and drew their students to them there. A complex and cooperative undertaking, during which grammars and dictionaries poured off the press and influenced one another between one edition and the next, was more what was going on. The nationalities of scholars and the material they worked on were often at variance—Rasmus Christian Rask was Danish, for example, and edited Icelandic sagas; Franz Bopp traveled from Bavaria to Paris to read ancient manuscripts brought from India[4]—and, of course, this heterogeneity illustrates the point. What was established was a network of correspondences transcending the boundaries of nations or of languages, beaming backwards into the past to set up new and demonstrable patterns. Philology could be seen as a kind of archeology dealing not with artifacts but with the words and the sounds of human speech as these appear in the mummified form of writing or in the more alive, though fleeting, sounds of the languages one hears in the streets.

Of the many workers in this enterprise Jacob Grimm is probably the best known today by virtue of two of his undertakings. He and his brother Wilhelm were led by their interest in comparative folklore to collect children's stories from many literatures, and these, translated in turn all over the globe, are known to millions with no particular background in philology as *Grimm's Fairy Tales*. A second of Grimm's linguistic achievements menaces today's student at a later phase than the fairy tales, sometimes with ogre-like effect, as "Grimm's Law," having to do with a shifting of consonants. A brief example may remind the reader of lore he has forgotten and will serve to show the quite commonsense physical basis for this kind of inquiry. In the initial consonants of the Latin *pater* and the English *father*, the sounds *p* and *f*, as the reader can check himself, are made in about the same part of the mouth, with a substitution of the upper teeth (*f*) for the upper lip (*p*). Grimm's Law (using "law" in the sense of pattern and predictability in human behavior) thus dealt specifically with certain stop-consonants in Indo-European, the basic family to which most European and many Asian languages belong. The "First Germanic Consonant Shift," which Grimm's Law describes, systematizes the movement from Indo-European into the Germanic subgroup to which English belongs as the following: Indo-European *p*, *t*, and *k* became Germanic *f*, *th*, and *h*; Indo-European *b*, *d*, and *g* became Germanic *f*, *t*, and *k*; and Indo-European *bh*, *dh*, and *gh* became Germanic *b*, *d*, and *g*.[5]

This small drop, a sample of a large linguistic bucket, enabled scholars to postulate components of lost and forgotten languages. Sequences could be worked out, family trees of languages could be drawn up; derivations could be understood, spellings could be seen as historical clues, and even place names could advance from a category of quaint curiosities to one of reliable scientific fact, capable of supplying long-lost knowledge about a geographical spot and its peoples. All this involved many discoveries besides Grimm's Law, and Grimm's Law itself is much more complex than has been indicated here. (It was not, in fact, entirely the work of Grimm but was based upon formulations by Rask.) But, however labelled, these observations had in the 1820s the effect of a galvanic shock. Grimm's statement that all trustworthy philological systems must henceforth be based upon rigorous adherence to the laws of sound change was recognized as a turning point. Philology could now become a science—coherent, systematic, its theories susceptible to proof.

Linguistic scholarship until this point in the early nineteenth century had been a slapdash affair in which similarities were noted and conclusions drawn with a kind of cheerful and creative spontaneity. One school of thought held that Hebrew must be the oldest and purest of languages, since so much of the Bible was written in it, and all the others must have somehow degenerated from this standard. Another school, looking at the Bible in more detail, found that God had created all the languages at one swoop to prevent the building of the Tower of Babel; that they were separate entities like the animals of the Garden of Eden; and that to postulate earlier origins or cross-relationships among the languages was quite as sacrilegious as to contemplate evolution among the species of animals. Many people, in other words, knew exactly where they stood with regard to philology. All this changed as the jigsaw puzzle began to fit together, and Germany, where the University of Berlin could boast both Bopp and Grimm on her faculty and where other universities were catching up fast, became a mecca for scholars of languages. To Americans, Germany had already become the place to go for advanced studies.[6] This choice was partly by default, as the universities of England limited the number of foreign students they were willing to admit, and Americans had to go somewhere until their own graduate programs got under way. But a greater influence on the American regard for German higher education was the latter's openness to new ideas and active encouragement of scholarship. German patterns were carried over into the developing American institutions; Thomas Jefferson made a special study of the German system while planning the University of Virginia in the early nineteenth century, and American graduate schools, as they were established, typically offered the Ph.D.—a German degree, not an English one. Among the many Americans who returned from their philological immersion in Germany to pursue the new specialty of English language and literature were Francis James Child of Harvard, who studied at Göttingen and Berlin; Child's successor and protégé, George Lyman Kittredge, Leipzig and Tübingen; and Albert S. Cook of Johns Hopkins and Yale, Göttingen and Leipzig.

Having learned Anglo-Saxon and perhaps Middle English, the student returning from Germany felt a natural urge to practice his skills on the real thing. Here the English had an advantage over the Americans. Piles of early manuscripts had been lying around England for centuries. Many had been mutilated or destroyed during the anti-Catholic fervor which accompanied the dissolution in the sixteenth century of the monasteries where the manuscripts had been kept and the Puritan regime of the seventeenth century, when writings having to do with saints or with any idolatrous embellishment of religion were persecuted once again. Of the manuscripts and early printed books which survived, written for the most part in Latin but occasionally in Anglo-Saxon or the various forms of Middle English, some had been well treated, kept among their owners' most treasured possessions, and eventually made available to scholars. Among the early collectors were Matthew Parker, mentioned above, whose library was given to Corpus Christi College, Cambridge; Sir Robert Cotton, many of whose books and manuscripts (including the Beowulf manuscript, damaged by fire in the meantime) went to the British Museum upon the latter's establishment in the eighteenth century; and Robert Harley, Earl of Oxford, whose immense library (50,000 printed books, 8,000 volumes of manuscripts) also became part of the British Museum's increasingly important collection.[7]

These men and others like them, "antiquaries" as they were called, set the stage for the development of English studies in more ways than merely assembling the materials, crucial as that contribution was. They pioneered an attitude of mind, a curiosity about and appreciation of the past, which was not widespread among the populace in their day and which sometimes let them in for ridicule. Some antiquaries were more intellectually inclined than others; a few, for example, learned to read their Anglo-Saxon manuscripts and published grammars of the language. Others were quite unspecialized. A country squire with antiquarian leanings might happily collect anything oldish that came his way—an Elizabethan broadside here, a Roman coin there. In speculating about their finds the latter type often produced exercises of the imagination untrammeled by fact or logic which, if published, were to enrage their intellectual heirs of the more scientific nineteenth century. Yet the antiquaries set a pattern of collecting things, learning about them, and keeping them in a safe place, without which English language and literature, and a number of other concerns as well, could not well have done.

The Early English Text Society

The existence of a manuscript was all to the good, especially if it were housed in a library or a private collection to which a scholar could gain access. But a manuscript could only be read by one person at a time, with any convenience, and larger numbers of people were feeling the attraction of early forms of the language. What was needed was a means to get the manuscript into print—accurately transcribed, provided with notes and glossary—and into the hands of those readers who were already interested in early English or who could be expected to become so. The solution was typically Victorian. If in the eighteenth century learning was furthered mainly by individuals, and in the twentieth century mainly by universities, the favorite agency in the nineteenth century, highly functional and often highly successful, was the "learned society."

The types of learning encouraged by these societies covered a wide spectrum between the sciences and the humanities, often incorporating both, and their membership was similarly varied. While some members might be university professors and other specialists, others were amateurs, men and occasional women of some education and considerable intellectual energy. The societies' aims often included the sponsorship of publications. In this category we find the Early English Text Society, which set out to get the materials for studying early English out of their isolated manuscripts and onto the bookshelves of the scholars who needed them.

This body was founded in 1865 in London, at the suggestion of Frederick James Furnivall (himself an indefatigable founder of societies), by the Philological Society, which can thus be seen as the parent of the E.E.T.S. The Philological Society had been founded in 1842, with originally an emphasis on classical philology which then expanded to the consideration of English. In this later pursuit it had set out to produce a new dictionary of the English language, arranged on historical principles, each word traced through the various forms it had taken during the centuries and illustrated at each phase with examples from contemporary documents. (The suggestion for the dictionary also came from Furnivall, in conjunction with a paper read by Richard C. Trench.) This ambitious project was to become in the fulness of time the mighty *Oxford English Dictionary*, which now sits so calmly on the reference shelves in the splendor of its many volumes and growing supplements that a passerby might think it had appeared with effortless dignity, an etymological Venus from the waves; the facts, of course, are quite different.[8]

In the early stages of the O.E.D., the hundreds of volunteer readers, combing book after book and making reference slips to illustrate the uses of words, discovered that texts from the Middle English period (roughly 1150 to 1500) were both insufficient in quantity and untrustworthy in form. Manuscripts were not easily accessible; printed texts made from the manuscripts, if such existed, were likely to have had their verbal forms altered to make them easier to understand. What was needed was a good supply of medieval texts, soundly edited, with nothing smoothed out—all the lumps left in, in other words, to add to the interest and authenticity. Thus the Early English Text Society faced a clear if strenuous task.

In taking as its objective the publication of a certain class of book

the E.E.T.S. was following a long tradition.[9] Matthew Parker had
organized in the sixteenth century the Elizabethan Society of Antiquaries for the publication of his prized Anglo-Saxon manuscripts, for
which endeavor a special font of Anglo-Saxon type had been cut. Another predecessor, the Roxburghe Club, was among the most elite of
the early nineteenth-century printing societies; its members were aristocratic or wealthy, usually both; and each was expected to have printed
at his own expense a rare book, usually one dating from the sixteenth
or even the fifteenth century, for distribution to the membership only.
In Scotland, Walter Scott in 1823 founded the Bannatyne Club in
Edinburgh to promote interest in Scottish antiquities and to publish
important books in the field. The Maitland Club in Glasgow, with
similar aims, soon followed.

Since the Early English Text Society had set out to make available
to a specialist readership those books which a commercial publisher
would hesitate to bring out because of the works' limited appeal, the
society of course had to guard against going broke itself. In other words,
it had to make sure the small quantity of books it printed would be
paid for, and this it did by charging an annual subscription. One guinea
(one pound and one shilling, or $42 by the rough and ready process
of turning nineteenth-century pounds into late twentieth-century dollars by multiplying by forty) entitled a member to a year's worth of
books, six to eight of them usually. An additional guinea would cover
a subscription to the "extra series" titles, edited from early printed books
rather than from the manuscripts which made up the "original series"
list. Printing costs were by present-day standards quite low and were
made even lower in this case by the fact that salaries to editors and
other volunteer workers were minimal to nonexistent.

The resulting row on row of volumes, numbering by the turn of
the century well over a hundred in the original series with the extra
series coming briskly along, have become the backbone of virtually
every academic library's early and Middle English collection.[10] They
present great variety. Since texts were selected for their philological as
well as their literary value, one finds fifteenth-century cookery books,
Anglo-Saxon riddles, fourteenth-century romances, legal records (Furnivall spent long hours in remote country libraries copying documents
on such matters as "Child Marriages, Divorces and Ratifications in the
Diocese of Chester"), medical treatises which can stand the hair of the

modern reader well on end, and the lives of some remarkably obscure saints—as well as such milestones of English literature as *Piers Plowman*, Chaucer's poems, *Sir Gawaine and the Green Knight*.

Among the many editors in this enterprise, besides Furnivall, were Richard Morris, whose long list of E.E.T.S. volumes begins with the society's first appearance in print, *Early English Alliterative Poems of the West Midland Dialect of the Fourteenth Century* ("copied and edited from a unique manuscript in the British Museum"); Henry Sweet, who edited *King Alfred's West Saxon Version of Gregory's Pastoral Care*; J. A. H. Murray, editor in chief of the *Oxford English Dictionary*, who found time to edit the *Romance and Prophecies of Thomas of Erceldoune*; and Walter William Skeat.

A noteworthy aspect of the Early English Text Society was its successful infiltration into the halls of learning. In view of the number of professors among the membership, this maneuver is perhaps not surprising, but it was ingenious. The Society needed members in general and editors in particular, and it managed both to identify and to reward a likely group of prospects by offering an annual prize, at a number of colleges and universities, to the student writing the best paper in a special examination in early English. The prizes (E.E.T.S. volumes) did not greatly set back the Society; students were given recognition and encouragement; and the preparation for the examination, which took place outside the official curriculum and involved professors' volunteering to give special lectures, helped make English studies a familiar phenomenon before more than a handful of universities had approved courses in it. (Henry Morley at University College, London, and David Masson at the University of Edinburgh were among many professors who made a special point of the E.E.T.S. prize.) Some of the questions set on these examinations appear rather on the minute side and may reflect the Society's preoccupation with the problems of editing: "What letters are most apt to be misread by copyists of early manuscripts? How are they misread, and why?" Others deal more intrinsically with historical and linguistic matters: "Ralph Higden distinguished three forms of the English spoken in his time; what were they? What peculiarity of inflection serves as the best test for ascertaining to which of these three forms an early English text belongs?" (These particular questions were set in 1866;[11] the examinations continued through the turn of the century.)

As the Early English Text Society gained fame, membership came to include persons and institutions who may not have devoted their lives to esoteric lore but who were interested in language and literature and who liked to see a job well done. The authors Alfred Tennyson and Anthony Trollope appear on the membership list, along with many other private persons and an increasing number of libraries. The Penzance Public Library and Trinity College Library, Cambridge, may serve as an indication of the spread here. The E.E.T.S. also developed a following overseas, especially in Ireland, Canada, and Australia, in all of which countries English studies took firm root by the end of the nineteenth century and blossomed in the twentieth. The Library of Congress in Washington got its regular volumes; so did Harvard, of course, with Francis James Child on the library committee. Considerable credit should be given to these subscribers, great and small. The E.E.T.S. depended on them for its success; one sympathizes with them, reading along as best they could, patiently forking out all those guineas and finding themselves sternly admonished from time to time by an anonymous voice (probably Furnivall's) from the endpapers of the latest arrival:

> The Subscribers to the Original Series must be prepared for the issue of the whole of the Early English *Lives of Saints*, sooner or later. The Society cannot leave out any of them, even though some are dull. The Sinners would doubtless be much more interesting. But in Saints' Lives will be found valuable incidental details of our forefathers' social state, and all are worthful for the history of our language. The Lives may be lookt on as the religious romances or story books of their period.[12]

The Modern Language Association of America

Meanwhile across the Atlantic, the study of English language and literature had taken a turn towards greater recognition in higher education with the founding in 1883 of the Modern Language Association. The first M.L.A. meeting took place during the Christmas holidays, a pause in the academic calendar which has retained its convenience for a century and more, at Columbia College (later Columbia University) in New York.[13] By the next year the locale had shifted to Johns Hopkins

University, in Baltimore; here the second meeting attracted forty charter members from twenty institutions including, besides Columbia and Johns Hopkins, Amherst, Boston University, Brown, Hamilton, Harvard, Lafayette, Lehigh, the University of Michigan, the University of Pennsylvania, Princeton, the University of St. Louis, Swarthmore, Syracuse, Tufts, Vanderbilt, the University of Virginia, Williams, and Yale.

The fact that all the modern languages, not just English but German and French as well, and Spanish and Italian, felt impelled to band together is perhaps an indication of their lowly place in the academic hierarchy, as they perceived the situation. Latin and Greek were not viewed as the enemy, exactly, but the newcomers felt that the curriculum might become a little more flexible. In the words of a paper read at the second annual meeting to an audience in which the speaker probably met with little dissent:

> The question is not, Must the classics go? nor is it the more specific question, must the Greek go? . . . The question is, will the classics as taught in our colleges make any concessions of their large amount of time to the modern languages?[14]

Edging into the magic circle of courses required for the undergraduate degree was one of the more grittily practical of the M.L.A.'s early concerns. Others were more theoretical. Programs for the annual meetings were listed first in the Association's *Proceedings* and soon in the *Publications of the Modern Language Association,* founded in 1885 and now known simply as *PMLA.* Here we find the earliest members pondering questions of pedagogy. What were the best teaching methods, the best exercises? What, exactly, should be taught in an English literature course? Many lists were proposed for the latter, and in some cases even the authors conceded that what they had drawn up was a syllabus not for a single year, but for three or four. A spirit of enthusiasm is everywhere present. Papers could be read to the entire body of delegates, for in the earliest days everyone present fitted easily into one lecture hall, and nobody would have dreamed of scheduling two papers at the same time. The process of specialization, moreover, had not yet driven professors of the modern languages into areas too remote for easy communication; and everyone was equipped to enjoy a paper on French dialects in Louisiana or allegory in Spenser, Bunyan, and Swift. Social events took place on a similarly small scale. In 1889, under the leadership of James Russell Lowell, the M.L.A. met at Harvard and was invited as a body to a reception in the home of the University president, Charles W. Eliot. The Association's annual dues, three dollars, might seem at first glance another instance of the M.L.A.'s small beginnings, but in fact this amount was considerable in terms of the buying power of the day. Three dollars in a restaurant would buy a good meal of many courses, and hotel rooms (those the M.L.A. recommended for its members, at any rate) cost $1.50.

In its early decades the M.L.A. retained its concern with pedagogical matters, but as the modern languages gained a firmer foothold in college curricula this concern relaxed somewhat, and the Association's emphasis shifted from teaching to research. (Pedagogy then became the province of professional organizations within the respective languages; the National Council of Teachers of English, for example, was founded in 1911.) M.L.A. membership in the 1880s was more evenly divided among the languages, English departments being at that time proportionately smaller. German professors were particularly well represented. German in fact remained a very popular course until the outbreak of the First World War, when America seemed to take the curious defensive stance that German culture did not exist and enrollment fell drastically. Women were slenderly represented in the M.L.A. of the nineteenth century, as was the case in the groves of academe generally. An exception was M. Carey Thomas, Professor of English and Dean of the Faculty at Bryn Mawr, who had pursued her career in the new subject with considerable determination. She took a B.A. at Cornell in 1877, then received permission to study for a Master's degree at Johns Hopkins, "without class attendance"; proceeding to Zurich, she earned a Ph.D. in 1882 *summa cum laude*. Hired at Bryn Mawr and determined to make it "as good as the best men's colleges and not another 'female seminary,'" she joined the M.L.A. as a professor from Bryn Mawr before the college actually opened, in 1885.[15]

In its concerns related to English language and literature, the M.L.A. often acted in harmony with its colleagues in Britain and elsewhere in the English-speaking world. Plans for simplified spelling were much talked of—a cause which has now been dormant for so long that it may rise up again any day, perhaps with more efficacy this time. Another basic attitude shared by English professors at this point in the development of the discipline was the necessity of Anglo-Saxon for a solid connection with the language. At the 1884 meeting, Henry

Wood of Johns Hopkins stated what would have been taken as an article in this creed: "Every person teaching English should thoroughly understand Anglo-Saxon, and should be able to answer the very practical questions of students, particularly as to the development of English sounds."[16]

By the turn of the century, membership in M.L.A. was slightly over five hundred, a quite respectable figure. (A hundred years after its founding the Association's directory was to list some 23,400-odd names and professorial addresses.) Despite some proposals in the 1890s of a merger with some of Canada's fast-growing learned societies, the M.L.A. remained a national association. A global perspective was characteristic, however. At its 1899 meeting the M.L.A. voted affirmatively on two matters sent to it by its British colleagues—to send greetings to Furnivall, whose seventy-fifth birthday was to be honored by the scholarly world, and to submit papers to the commemoration of the thousandth anniversary of the death of King Alfred, to be observed in the summer of 1901 in Winchester.

The Education of the Masses

The Modern Language Association had not shifted its attention away from teaching because it found the matter unimportant but because so many other groups and individuals were deeply involved with it; research in fact was the aspect of the discipline that needed help. This unprecedented growth at all levels of the educational establishment affected language study in general and English study in particular, in both the United States and Britain.

Two groups in the population were especially affected by the new educational energy, the young and the working class. The latter category was not really very large, comparatively speaking, but it was substantial enough to sow the seeds for greater things.[17] The various mechanics' institutes in the industrial cities of northern England established reading rooms and sponsored lectures, and when their communities began to found municipal universities—often by pulling together whatever educational establishments already existed—the mechanics' institutes frequently became an important ingredient. The Working Men's College in London, where Furnivall taught English for many years, was founded in 1854 and offered instruction in a surprisingly large variety of subjects to students who already held full-time jobs. [18] Instruction in English, here as elsewhere, was to a large extent practical, with emphasis upon letter writing; but literature had a definite place. The best way to build a habit of reading, after all, was to give the students something to read. And the appeal of English literature to the students' patriotic and moral sense was a strong one—the more so since these schools often drew strongly upon the country's education-oriented Nonconformist element.

It was the establishment of free public schools for children ("public" in the American sense of being supported by public funds and open to all within a given locality) that gave English studies its biggest numerical boost. In England, various acts of Parliament (in particular the Education Act of 1870) illuminated the evolving ideal of universal education; in the United States, where education is the responsibility of the states rather than of the federal government, a complex pattern of local school districts, state supervisory authorities, and boards (both elected and appointed) had in common, despite their differences, inefficiencies and biases, a deep fundamental concern for the education of the country's future citizens. And in both England and America legislation was passed setting up special institutions (sometimes given the rather chilling label of "normal schools") to train the teachers who were in turn to train the children. Many of these schools went on in the twentieth century to merge with, or become, liberal arts colleges. The English departments, installed since the beginning, made the jump without difficulty.

The esteem given English literature as a component of the elementary and secondary school curricula on both sides of the Atlantic might perhaps be seen as a coincidence in the respective development of the two countries. John H. Fisher, in a recent article, suggests two reasons for the acceptance of literature as an academic subject. A literature may be studied "out of reverence for the civilization it embodies, which is accepted as superior to the civilization of those studying."[19] At a later point, "when nationalism or some narrower form of ethnocentricity rears its head, the native literature is resurrected, refurbished, and reinterpreted as a means of defining the national character." Perhaps, then, England went through the first phase by establishing classical literature as a discipline and then in the nineteenth century reached the second phase, just when the United States, on the same timetable with regard to the political and moral idealism which helped establish the public school systems but on a later one with regard to its own nationalism, was ready to decide what literature was worthy of study. "English literature," Fisher points out from the American perspective, "became our archetypal literature, providing models of expression and sophistication for American students just as Virgil and Cicero had provided models for students in France and England from the sixth century to the sixteenth."[20]

In defense of America one cannot help observing that the country managed to reach its nationalistic phase quite energetically in the twentieth century, becoming a land of Faulkner specialists overnight, and that Latin was not replaced by English literature but was greatly esteemed and was a taken-for-granted requirement for college entrance. Furthermore, with the exception of a handful of very special works, until the twentieth century America simply didn't have very much in the way of literature, at least to compare with England's array. These things take time and other resources.

In both countries, in any case, students from social strata which had not had much to do with schools now sat dutifully in rows, undergoing the remarkably systematic education suddenly devised to cope with them. Routine was important. Students and teachers needed a sense of stability. It was important, too, that students be able to see some immediate value in what they were learning, and here literature in its moralistic (indeed, didactic) aspects came in very handy. The deliciousness of literature is not universally apprehended in an elementary classroom, but the sense that one is imbibing wisdom which is esteemed by one's elders and which will become apparent at some future point if not at the present moment is, somehow, more easily transferable. Pupils recited Gray's "Elegy," learned with Macbeth that the rewards of ambition can turn into the sere and yellow leaf, and rejoiced with Keats at the timelessness of beauty—experiences which however old-fashioned or quaint they may seem today, nevertheless often stayed with the pupils all their lives and patterned their interpretations of reality.

Shakespeare in the Nineteenth Century

In the educational hierarchy, Shakespeare was pervasive from bottom to top, from the elementary school pupil reciting "This above all, to thine own self be true" before his assembled friends and family at Class Day, to his prospective teacher writing a comparison of Rosalind and Portia on her way to a teaching certificate at the state Normal School, to *her* prospective teacher working away at a major university, reading Seneca in the original but also concerned with the survival of Middle English pronouns in *King Lear*. Outside this busy pyramid and its proliferation of jobs for students of English literature were large numbers of Shakespeare enthusiasts who had nothing to do with formal education, or nothing to do with the teaching part of it at any rate. These last categories include actors and theater managers, Baconians, editors of Shakespearean texts, librarians, founders and members of learned societies, trustworthy scholars, scholars whose actions are suspect, bibliographers, and many others.

The Baconian phenomenon need detain us only briefly. None of the four scholars with whom we are chiefly concerned took this movement with any seriousness (with the possible exception of Child, whose usually calm demeanor gave way to rage when the subject was mentioned). But the Baconian theory demonstrates the extent to which the nineteenth century saw Shakespeare as a sort of recreation ground, a common cultural holding to which all were welcome. The Baconians' basic assumption, that Shakespeare's plays are too varied, complex and generally miraculous to have been written by one man, or at any rate by one man relatively lacking in formal education, is at bottom somewhat flattering to the author. The claim that the plays had been written by Shakespeare's contemporary Francis Bacon was first made in the eighteenth century but came to prominence in the nineteenth, particularly in the writings of one Delia Bacon, an American who spent several years in England researching *The Philosophy of the Plays of Shakespeare Unfolded,* published in 1857. Francis Bacon, Walter Raleigh, and Edmund Spenser were the triumvirate proposed by Miss Bacon as the true authors. In 1885 the Baconian Society was founded in England to promote this and similar suggestions, and about the same time, several American seekers worked out and published evidence of secret anagrams and ciphers purportedly scattered about the texts by Bacon as a sort of signature. These discoveries caused recurrent sensations.[21] Even today, no one who teaches Shakespeare can expect to escape being asked about the matter (the public seems to feel there is something professors are not telling), and one might as well accept such queries as evidence of the deep hold Shakespeare has in our culture.

Another of the nineteenth century's Shakespearean tempests was a more serious affair and one which affected the world of literary study much more deeply; to a scholar the crime of forgery is a crime against the pursuit of truth and evokes a kind of horror mixed with bafflement: Why did he do it? The motives in this case remain obscure. John Payne Collier, founder of the Shakespeare Society in London in 1841, may have had fame as his object; but as he had already become a respected scholar without the help of forged evidence, it is hard to see why he yielded to the urge. Several literary investigators have suggested that Collier simply had a gambler's temperament and that his motives are consequently not aligned with logical expectations. That he had written marginal annotations in a copy of the Shakespeare second folio and then used these purportedly seventeenth-century annotations to support editorial theories of his own was established to the satisfaction of both the scholarly and the general public in 1859. By this point his Shakespeare Society, which had published some forty volumes of primary material for the study of Shakespeare (including Gosson's *School of Abuse*), had disbanded in disgrace. (No other members were implicated.) With the ruin of Collier's reputation went that of his previous bibliographical and scholarly work, much of it concerned with Shakespeare. The affair caused repercussive waves of personal bitterness and subsidiary quarrels, for many people became involved in the controversy, and friendships were impaired or broken. Perhaps as an indication that such a case should not be declared permanently closed, Collier has been defended in a recent investigation by Dewey Ganzel, whose *Fortune and Men's Eyes: The Career of John Payne Collier* delves closely into the documents and examines the motives for disparaging Collier of various habitués of the British Museum Reading Room in the 1850s.[22]

In 1873, twenty years after the dissolution of Collier's Shakespeare Society, Furnivall founded the New Shakspere Society for the purpose of determining the chronological sequence of the plays. (Furnivall insisted on the spelling. Spelling was not standardized in Shakespeare's day, and the poet himself spelled his own name without regard for consistency.) As with so many of the ground-breaking projects of the nineteenth century, this one is hard for the present-day reader to visualize in its original excitement. Once again, we are spoiled by the reference material which we have at our fingertips and can take for granted. The chronology of the plays, by now thoroughly investigated, appears in tabular form in many collected editions of Shakespeare's works, often with lists of sources should one wish to follow through the arguments. But for Furnivall and his colleagues, collecting evidence of this sort was a new adventure. Particularly new was the application of internal stylistic tests, such as the counting-up of end rhymes, and it was this sort of thing which outraged some segments of the Victorian public, unaccustomed to subjecting works of genius to arbitrary measurement. Once again, Shakespeare became a center of turbulence, for Furnivall was unable to resist a fight. His opponent in this case was the poet Algernon Charles Swinburne; the quarrel enlivened the press with letters, accusations, rebuttals, and an exercise in name-calling which cannot be described as dignified. Members of the New Shakspere Society began to steal away in embarrassment, and the organization was disbanded in 1892.

Yet another Shakespeare Society, this one in Philadelphia, sponsored a substantial contribution to the growing shelf of Shakespearean reference works. The project, begun in 1871, was the fourth *Variorum Shakespeare*; the editor was Horace Howard Furness, a Harvard graduate of 1854 who abandoned his law career in order to pursue his literary interests. Each *Variorum* volume contains not only the text of its play with its many and complex variants, but masses of critical commentary as well, arranged for easy line-by-line reference. While from today's perspective such commentary is often far from up-to-date, it is accessible and often surprisingly useful. The *Variorum* outlived Furness's editorship and that of his son, H. H. Furness, Jr. Since the 1930s the *Variorum* has been conducted by the Modern Language Association, under whose auspices the last few volumes continue to appear.

Editing of Shakespearean texts, as of literary texts in general, took great leaps forward in the nineteenth century. Among the brightest of the constellation is the *Cambridge Shakespeare*, the first volume of which appeared in 1863. The second edition, which came out between 1891 and 1893, was the work of Aldis Wright, librarian of Trinity College, Cambridge. Wright had taken a substantial part in the first edition as well, sharing the job with John Glover and William George Clark. The nine-volume Cambridge edition is the parent of the one-volume *Globe* Shakespeare, much used since its appearance in 1864. Despite his literary expertise and his long connection with Cambridge, Wright never held a teaching position, a discrepancy which probably seems larger to us today than it did to Wright's contemporaries. The role of English literature in academia grew very slowly at Cambridge, and editing Shakespeare was seen as something one could do for its own sake.

Meanwhile, the Victorian public went on enjoying its Shakespeare in its own way. The lavishness characteristic of the nineteenth-century stage spread happily into the Shakespearean repertoire. Titania and Oberon could have a complete forest, with ferns and bosky dells and a distant waterfall (layers of gauze shaken up and down by the stage-hands); Shylock could stalk through an elaborate Venetian canalscape, all lacy arches diminishing in perspective like a Renaissance painting, enlivened by moving gondolas; Antony and Cleopatra dominated respectively a Rome and an Egypt of massive pillars, bevies of dancing girls, ranks of soldiers on review. Lavishness also extended to acting talent, self-confident and intensely personal, which often ran in families. The Keans, the Kembles, the Trees, singly or in groups, won enthusiastic followings in Britain and made triumphant tours of America, where thousands saw Fanny Kemble as Juliet or Ellen Terry as Lady Macbeth.

This approach to drama in general and Shakespeare in particular has its advantages. The emphasis on spectacle made the theater a magic place, palpably different from everyday reality, and people wanted to go to it. If Shakespeare's lines were hard to follow, there was always something else to notice. And, since no one objected to seeing the same play over and over (though usually in different productions), the lines of the text might sink in eventually. We can assume that a fairly large proportion of future literary scholars made their earliest contact with Shakespeare in the form of a family excursion to the theater, enjoyed by all.

A disadvantage of the nineteenth-century's elaborate staging, of course, was the harm done to the play as a coherent entity. Shakespeare had written for an essentially bare stage, where actors moved briskly on and off and carried the plot along with them. Dropping a curtain to take Troy away and bring on the Greek camp paralyzed the action and lost, besides momentum, dozens of delicious little parallels and ironies which Shakespeare built into his plays through the quick juxtaposition of scenes. The text was also altered by cuts made to allow time for all the scenery-shifting and by out-and-out revisions; happy endings for *King Lear* and *Romeo and Juliet* really occurred and left most of the audience cheerfully unaware of the different and larger experience intended for them by the playwright.

Despite these irregularities, it is hard to condemn the Victorians for enjoying their Shakespeare. A positive public attitude toward any segment of literature is refreshing. And Victorian enthusiasm has left numerous legacies—the theatrical venture at Stratford-upon-Avon, for example, established in the 1870s and now one of the homes of the Royal Shakespeare Company—which today's sterner and more complicated theatrical theories can build upon. Nineteenth-century enthusiasm for Shakespeare has benefited the world of letters as well as the world of the theater; in America the energetic devotion of Standard Oil executive Henry Clay Folger resulted in the collection that eventually became the Folger Shakespeare Library in Washington, D.C.

English Studies, Past and Future

As the Shakespearean scene both theatrical and textual and as many of the topics treated in the foregoing pages would seem to indicate, the birth of English studies in the universities in the late nineteenth century did not come as an isolated phenomenon. Learned men and women had been turning their attention to these materials for some time, but in contexts other than academic ones.

The eighteenth century saw the emergence of the "man of letters" as a new figure in society, dependent for financial support upon pleasing not an aristocratic patron but an increasingly literate public. Speaking particularly of literary criticism, Walter Scott Achtert finds that this period "afforded the man of letters a new dignity and new and wider avenues for criticism—new periodicals, clubs, and coffeehouses, and a prosperous middle class seriously interested in 'culture.'"[23] Joseph Addison's series of articles on *Paradise Lost*, appearing in the *Spectator* in 1711 and 1712, are an example here. The nineteenth century was to bring a proportionately much larger reading public, but the roots were set out with these earlier beginnings.

Besides periodicals, the eighteenth century and its public encouraged the writing of English dictionaries, of which the most famous was Samuel Johnson's in 1755, and of literary history, of which Thomas Warton's *History of English Poetry* in 1774–81 was an impressive if not always reliable example. William Hazlitt and Charles Lamb in the early nineteenth century wrote of English literature—Renaissance drama, for instance—with appreciation and perception, employing sometimes the tone of explorers; they seemed to assume their readers would find their observations interesting but could hardly be expected to have read the works themselves. Since so much of English literature was not in print in the first quarter of the century, this assumption was perfectly realistic.

Of the men of letters active during the time when English studies had begun to invade the universities, two fairly representative examples have already appeared in this chapter in varying lights. John Payne Collier we need not rake over the coals again, but it might be pointed out that his occupations—journalist, theater critic, literary historian, editor, bibliographer, librarian—are typical of the man earning a living by his pen. Collier had in fact been educated as a lawyer, as was also the case with another scholar whose appearance in these pages have been and will continue to be frequent, Frederick James Furnivall. This personage, wildly energetic even by Victorian standards, practiced law infrequently at the beginning of his career but soon gave up even that to devote himself to English language and literature.[24] His editing jobs paid him slender sums, and his teaching at the Working Men's College added another pittance, but his life was not luxurious and could hardly be called even comfortable; indeed, the fact that some men of letters were able to live reasonably well by their wits can hardly be taken as an assurance that they all did. The literate public seemed willing to pay for some things more than others, as is the case today, and Middle English texts were apparently not very high on the list.

Three more representative Victorian men of letters will complete this demonstration of the variety of the species and of their relevance to English as an emerging academic discipline. John Churton Collins wanted to become an English professor as soon as the job was invented and did the best he could as a university extension lecturer, eventually—near the end of his career—becoming head of the English Department at the University of Birmingham. In the meantime he carried on as a man of letters. He edited numerous reprints of English literary texts, wrote biographies and essays, and furthered controversies in the learned reviews. The Reverend Alexander Balloch Grosart was a Scot and a Presbyterian minister, preparing editions of English literature in his spare time, whose life might have been paralleled by David Masson had not Masson decided against a clerical career and eventually become an English professor instead. The role of the clergyman/scholar in the development of English studies is perhaps appropriate, since so many of the Anglo-Saxon and Middle English manuscripts were preserved in the monasteries. Finally, Leslie Stephen, rememberd today as editor of the *Dictionary of National Biography* (and as the father of Virginia Woolf) but in his own time the center of a whirlwind of literary activities and a highly respected critic and heavyweight journalist, achieved the kind of authoritative public image which the English professors were to strive for, more or less successfully.

Another component of the cultural matrix in which English studies were to thrive was the growth in the nineteenth century of public and private libraries. The British Museum will be briefly described in chapter four below, since David Masson once wrote a guide to it; the ancient university libraries—the Bodleian at Oxford, the University Library at Cambridge—had been in place for centuries when scholars began to investigate the treasures of their English manuscripts. Librarians were often scholars as well. Henry Bradshaw and Aldis Wright, both of Cambridge, are mentioned in these pages, and Frederic Madden, Keeper of the Manuscripts at the British Museum from 1833 until his death forty years later, distinguished himself in philology and paleology and edited a number of early English works, in particular Layamon's *Brut*. Libraries in the United States had naturally less of a head start with regard to acquisitions. The building up of collections in English literature, when such projects got under way in the late nineteenth and early twentieth centuries, naturally necessitated buying books and manuscripts from England as the early ones could hardly be obtained anywhere else. A consequent ambivalence is noticeable on the part of the English scholars who sometimes tend to feel that America has taken an undue advantage of her economic upswings by outbidding the English for their own cultural artifacts and then carting them away out of reach. This matter touches on too many other concerns to be answerable here—one might end up pointing to the Elgin Marbles or suggesting that imperialists have to take turns—and a more relevant point regarding the effect of good libraries upon English studies is the development on both sides of the Atlantic of sound, sensible techniques in library science. Materials are safely kept, accurately catalogued, made accessible to readers in a manner both hospitable and consistent with the principles of distributive justice, and all this progress has been built to a large extent upon the idealism and the energy of the librarians' Victorians forebears.

The Victorians produced an astonishing amount of work. By the end of the nineteenth century they had found, edited, and published virtually the entire canon of English literature; they had created dictionaries, concordances, and other tools necessary for scholarship, all of them made by hand; they had mapped out the history of English literature and filled in much of the interior details. Additions, variations, and new perspectives have been undertaken since; but the Victorians provided the framework. In higher education, the study of English language and literature had by the early twentieth century been accepted as essential to the English-speaking heritage, a basic humanistic discipline. Its practitioners were many and growing. The four scholars whose careers will be followed in this book had by this time achieved a place of high respect, while their students (and students' students), following at some chronological remove, established their own homesteads in the newly charted but largely unoccupied territory.

With so many of the basic tools in existence—and with some of them already beginning to be taken for granted—the new subject was ready for its professors to metamorphose from scholars into critics. This is what next occurred. In the first few decades of the twentieth century a new expectation arose of the English specialist; he was now assumed to possess not only knowledge but a theory. Frequently, as the century progressed it was literary criticism, rather than the literature itself, which was actually taught. (A rationale here, of course, was that the literature itself has already been part of the curriculum at some earlier stage of the educational process; English literature had after all become ubiquitous.) Students might be issued a single critical perspective on the grounds that it was the best one, or might be exercised more or less evenly upon several. Certainly schools of criticism multiplied vigorously as new discoveries and new disciplines shed their various lights over the traditional world of letters. Freud and Jung led to new views of the functions of comedy and tragedy, and of patterns of imagery; anthropology formed a partnership with linguistics to do tantalizing things with language studies. Historical events did their part in refocusing the boundaries and objectives of English studies. The First

World War brought about a concern for ultimate values just as the new discipline, her literary canon established, was ready to emphasize critical theory; subsequent historical events, in particular the century's wild leaps of science and technology with their effects upon human life individual and collective, gave to English studies as well as to other aspects of our culture a curiosity about and a frequently positive attitude toward fragmentation, multiplicity, and rapid change. Like the four gentlemen whose accomplishments we will next consider, today's English scholars tend to look ahead as well as backward; and our view of our discipline as well as our world is more optimistic, usually, than not. Perhaps this optimism results from our awareness of the vicissitudes through which English language and literature have already come. To this kind of awareness Morley, Child, Masson, and Skeat were happy to contribute.

2

Henry Morley (1822–1894), University College, and Literary History

Today, well over 150 years into its history, London's University College tends to chuckle over its early nickname, "The Godless Institution of Gower Street." But in the 1820s the name grew from popular indignation and general astonishment. Everything about the proposed endeavor seemed to contradict standard practice.[1] To set up a center of higher learning open to any student, regardless of religious label? To follow the German model of a professorial structure, rather than the Oxford/Cambridge tutorial one? And to finance itself not by waiting for some wealthy benefactor to establish a foundation but by incorporating itself as a joint stock company and actually offering shares to the public at so many pounds per share? Heads wagged.

The religious question had perhaps the most far-reaching implications. In the 1820s, when University College came into being, Oxford and Cambridge served only the sons of the ruling classes, a criterion distinguishable not through money but through religion. A student had to affirm his adherence to the articles of belief held by the Church of England. This requirement barred not only Catholics and Jews but many Protestants as well, Presbyterians to Baptists or what have you, collectively known as Nonconformists or as Dissenters because they dissented from the established church. This exclusivity had originated in the seventeenth century, when keeping all the power well centered between the Catholic extreme on the one hand and the Puritan extreme on the other could be seen as having some justification. The Catholic plotter Guy Fawkes came fairly close to blowing up James I and his Parliament in 1605, having filled the cellars of the Houses of Parliament with gunpowder; while the Puritan element, more organized and more effective, first packed Parliament not with explosives but with their party representatives, then fought against the

King's forces in the English Civil War, and eventually beheaded the King, Charles I, in 1649. The Act of Uniformity of 1662, passed when the Royalists got back into power, barred Dissenters from rearming themselves literally, economically, or intellectually, among these restrictions being that against attending either university.

But by the nineteenth century the Dissenters had simmered down to become useful segments of society, no threat to the Royal Family, unlikely to betray the country to outside invaders, and the barriers were gradually lowered. Even Cambridge and Oxford came round eventually; by 1900 the discriminatory Test Acts were no longer applied at either. Long before that time, of course, University College had been recognized as a successful experiment.

The nineteenth century was an era of growth in this category as in others. London's need for institutions of higher education was especially acute. University College opened in 1828, to be followed a few years later by King's College, which offered courses similar to those of University College but made a point of its ties with the Church of England.[2] Full-time faculty at King's College were in fact required to be members of the established church, although instructors of evening classes might range more widely among the nation's religious options.

In the 1830s, after a great deal of debate about the relationships of the growing number of new institutions and about the need for high and uniform educational standards, the University of London was created as something of an abstract entity, empowered to hold examinations and to grant degrees to students from a number of London institutions. University College students, whether studying law, medicine, or the liberal arts, sat for the University of London examinations, as did the students of King's College. (Some confusion may result from the name "University of London," as it was applied in the late 1820s to the institution which in fact became University College. The terminology sorted itself out quickly and need not detain us.) In the early twentieth century an administrative revision was to make the University of London a teaching institution by giving it a more direct supervision over the federation of schools and colleges under its wings. This array of educational enterprises has become an impressive one. The University of London now comprises, to name a very few, Bedford College (one of the earlier ones, founded in 1849 for women), the Courtauld Institute of Art, the London School of Economics and Political Science, and an increasing number of medical schools and specialist institutions. Since the 1930s, the University of London has had buildings of its own in Bloomsbury, not far from those of University College and in fact mixed in with them.

The area has not changed greatly, granted the increased height of most of the buildings and the increased velocity of the automobile over the horse. But the British Museum is still around the corner; the leafy squares of Bloomsbury still impart a sense of youth and growth; and the students of University College still hurry into the main building with its classical dome and pediment, originally of course the only building, designed in 1828 by William Wilkins (the architect as well of London's National Gallery) and restored after severe bomb damage in the Second World War.

The First Department of English

It was the intent of the founders (among them the liberal reformer Lord Brougham and the father of Utilitarianism, Jeremy Bentham) to offer a curriculum more in tune with the needs of the time than could be found at Cambridge or Oxford, where tradition tended to stifle innovation. Thus English Language and Literature was seen as worthy of a professorship—the first of its kind in higher education unless certain chairs of rhetoric (affiliated often with the study of philosophy and particularly with logic) or in belles lettres (dealing with the literature of other languages as well as English) were to be counted. It is in fact very hard to draw a line. One can say in any case that the authorities at University College gave considerable thought to what they were establishing, and to what they named it, and were not floating along haphazardly. Everything about University College was based on conscientious planning. King's College, which shared this zeal for working out details, put the new subject into a slightly different pigeonhole and several years later founded a chair of English History and Literature.

Designing an ideal University College was one thing, but implementing these designs was something else, and compromise was often in order. The College's attempts to attract professors provide a case in point. The authorities would have liked to bring in the leading scholars in each discipline, but salaries were a problem. Shares had not sold as well as had been projected, and the College's early years involved various types of budgetary derring-do. (Near the close of the century the

College finances were reorganized in a more traditional pattern, and the selling of shares became a thing of the past.)

In this atmosphere of innovation, idealism, and occasional backing and filling, some departments fared better than others. The English Department at first did rather badly. The first appointment, that of the Reverend Thomas Dale, seems to have been the result of internal politicking of a religious nature, a curious development in an institution devoted to religious freedom. Nevertheless, certain supporters had to be appeased, certain checks and balances set up, extensions in one quarter had to be repaid by contractions in another—putting a college together from scratch is after all a complex and uneven business. Dale, whose academic effectiveness varied according to the standard by which it was measured from minimal to mediocre, appears to have got the job because of his high moral stance. English literature, he declared in his inaugural speech, could make itself useful by serving the cause of morality. With this object in view, the literature studied by the young should be judiciously selected, in some cases expurgated; and some writers (Byron, for example) should be banned from the students' experience altogether.[3] From today's perspective, Dale's emphasis seems quite dismaying, and one is relieved to find that he remained at his post for only two years. Nevertheless, it might be fair to observe that the tendency to value literature in general and English literature in particular for its alleged ability to inculcate high moral principles was a common one in the nineteenth century. All four of the scholars with whom we shall be concerned held this view, expressing themselves with less rigidity than Dale and seeing the positive more than the negative aspects of the process of choosing literary works to be taught. One could not say that the tendency has disappeared today, or indeed that it is wholly reprehensible. One's own ideas of the good, the true, and the beautiful tend to appear self-evidently worthy of amplification. It is perhaps the narrowness of Dale's impulses at which one looks askance, rather than the impulses themselves.

Meanwhile at University College, subsequent professors of English continued to enact a scene familiar in academia, the procession of appointees who are brought in with high hopes all round, but who somehow don't work out. There was Robert Gordon Latham, about whom tradition records a social occasion ending with Latham, helplessly drunk, sliding from his chair to lie mumbling on the hearthrug. There was the poet Arthur High Clough (perhaps best known today for the wry irony of "The Latest Decalogue": "Thou shalt have one God only; who / Would be at the expense of two?"), whose general discontent and whose reluctance to dispense factual tidbits of use to his students on their examinations must have borne out some of the earliest professorial forebodings against creative writers in the English Department. ("They lack patience, you know.") At last, in the early 1850s, David Masson accepted the job, and University College was on its way at last to the kind of preeminence of which the founders felt the subject was capable. Masson lectured memorably and in general represented the college with distinction. The result, ironically, was that he was pursued by other institutions, and in the mid-1860s he returned to his native Scotland as Professor of Rhetoric and English Literature at the University of Edinburgh.

Enter Professor Morley

Henry Morley accepted the post in 1865, to remain for the next twenty-five years. University College became his life, sharing his affections only with his love for English literature and his love for his family. He was the solid, reliable professor which every academic department needs somewhere in its development, and Morley's aura of dependable authority was beneficial as well to the new discipline he professed.

Like many of his fellow enthusiasts in English studies, Morley was of middle-class background, the son of a surgeon.[4] It may be worth noting that medical practitioners in nineteenth-century England did not necessarily enjoy a high social status. A surgeon, for example, is not to be pictured as a masked figure in white doing dextrous things at an operating table; in the days before anesthesia or antiseptic procedures, operations were rare and dreadful occasions, and the surgeon's bread and butter was more in the line of setting broken bones and poulticing bruises. Morley's father was fortunate enough to gain a fair degree of success first in London, where Henry was born in 1822, and then in Kennington, at that time not a part of the London urban area but a small village south of the Thames.

Morley's early life combined extremes of grief and joy, terror and bliss in a mixture that might be called Dickensian; one thinks of *David Copperfield*, and one wonders if the fifteen years Morley spent in association with Dickens, as a writer for *Household Words* and *All the*

Year Round, might have influenced the way Morley himself remembered and described his childhood. On the other hand, Morley's experiences, some of which appeared in *Household Words,* may have influenced Dickens. Such speculations are probably frivolous. Certainly the nineteenth century provided enough childhood privation to go around. Morley's mother died when her son was barely two; with his older brother, Morley was sent to a succession of schools, one of which appars to have been particularly dreadful by way of internal warfare among the boys and a kind of class warfare of boys against masters. More or less in spite of themselves, the schools taught Morley some Latin and Greek. English literature was not taught as such, but Morley read Shakespeare's plays and Scott's novels as a private indulgence and perhaps as something of an escape.

Abruptly, when Morley was not quite eleven, his father decided to send him to Germany, to a school kept by the Moravian Brethren at Neuwied on the Rhine, not far from Bonn. The Moravian ideas of education were quite different from those prevalent in England. These gentle followers of the Sermon on the Mount taught and lived ideals of simplicity and of joy in learning. Preferring to influence other Christians rather than to raid their neighbors' churches and thus swell their own sectarian numbers, they opened their schools to all comers and set them up throughout Germany and eventually in England and America.

Here, picking up German quite easily, Morley spent two years, "the happiest portion of my life," as he records in his autobiographical *Early Papers and Some Memories* (1891). "In a school where quarrels were unknown, the masters were called Brothers, and all was canopied over with a veil of the tenderest and kindest religion, I spent my time laughing and loving everybody." This experience, coming to Morley just when he needed it, gave him the impetus at two of the several subsequent turnings of his life to choose education as the thing he wanted to do.

On his return to England (having suddenly become homesick; he was, after all, by then only thirteen), Morley spent several years in schools in and around London before taking up his medical education at the newly opened King's College. Morley's father had decided that one of his sons should follow in his footsteps, and Henry was a better student than his brother. Henry himself was not consulted on the matter of his career, nor did anyone seem to think he should have been—

an omission which Morley later recalls with some surprise, having by then survived into an age of more liberal relationships between parents and children. On completing his formal studies, Morley continued the usual sequence of training with a year's apprenticeship to a medical practitioner. Here he learned to ride in order to visit his rural Somerset patients, and here, in moments of leisure, he returned to his favorite works of English literature.

Morley's new professional step brings us to another episode of Dickensian misfortune. To set up on one's own, it was customary to buy a medical practice, or a partnership in a practice; and Morley, with the advice and financial help of his father, invested in a partnership in Shropshire. The senior partner then proved to be a fraud and a villain—"a gray headed Archimago," as Morley recalled in *Early Papers*—who eventually disappeared, not quite on the wings of the wind, but as definitively as if he had, taking with him the remains of Morley's purchase money and abandoning the miscellaneous debts and lawsuits in which he had been enmeshed. Investigation showed that Archimago had kept chaotic books and had no right to claim the high value he had put on the practice; further investigation showed that he was not legally qualified to practice in the first place.

Morley was thus stranded. He could not afford to move away; his impoverished patients could not pay him; his father could give him no further financial help. Worst of all, his poverty meant he could not marry the young lady, Mary Anne Sayer of the Isle of Wight, whom he had met through mutual friends and to whom he had been engaged for the past several years.

Relief came in the form of a cholera epidemic which brought a prospective buyer of the practice onto the scene. Morley sold it, without misrepresenting its value, for barely enough money to pay his traveling expenses, and then decided to abandon medicine as well as Shropshire and become a schoolmaster instead. Retrospectively, this decision seems an understandable one, but his own family and that of Miss Sayer were outraged. Mrs. Sayer felt at the end of her tether; her daughter had now been engaged for five years to a man who was as far from providing an adequate home for her as he had been at the beginning. She determined to break the engagement, forbade correspondence, and forced the lovers to secret strategems. For his part, Morley's father was angry because his son had given up not only his own profession but his own religion; attempting to argue Miss Sayer out of her family's Unitarian faith and into the Church of England, Morley had written a series of letters which had the effect as he wrote of reversing his own opinions.

By becoming a schoolmaster, Morley meant not the seeking of employment under someone else but the setting up of his own school, putting into practice the humane, child-oriented and by our own standards quite modern system of which he had been so fortunate a beneficiary at Neuwied on the Rhine. He went about his project with some commonsense. London, he felt, was too crowded an arena; the industrial cities of the north, fast-growing and full of life, seemed to offer a better chance, and here, in the town of Liscard, near Liverpool, Morley found parents who were willing to take a chance on a new kind of education for their sons and daughters. He leased a house, outfitted a downstairs room as a classroom, and started in, undertaking all the instruction himself in Latin, mathematics, history and geography, and, not surprisingly, English literature. As always, his energy was astonishing. His pupils liked their school and their master, and they learned what he taught them.

In this career Morley might have continued, expanding the school, hiring assistants, and reaching eventually a plateau of prosperity which would have allowed him to marry Miss Sayer, waiting all this time, two hundred miles south on the Isle of Wight, and clandestinely corresponding with Morley through sympathetic friends. But fate intervened, once again in the form of a cholera epidemic. Morley's medical training gave him an interest in public health, a matter which became topical whenever an epidemic threatened. Finding himself with some leisure one evening, Morley dashed off a treatise, in an ironic though factual vein, which he called "How to Make Home Unhealthy." It appeared in John Forster's monthly magazine *The Examiner*—a basically middle- to upper-middle-class publication, on the serious side, dealing with important issues of the day; Morley had sent his article there because he admired the magazine and in fact subscribed to it.

Thus Morley found himself with a new vocation. He was asked for more articles and supplied them, working even later into the night, for of course he continued to teach. At last, in 1851, came a letter from Charles Dickens, a close friend of Forster's and by that time an admirer of Morley's work: Morley was invited to move to London, to become a staff writer for Dickens's newly founded weekly magazine, *Household Words.*

A Journalist in London

The decision was a difficult one, for Morley has seen his school as his life work. At the same time, there were many opportunities in this new role as man of letters. *Household Words,* of course, need not take up all his time; he might undertake other writing projects simultaneously. But most of all, Dickens's offer meant he would make enough money (five guineas a week) to marry Miss Sayer, by this time a fiancée of nine years' standing—not a record for Victorian engagements, in a period when the groom's ability to support what seems by our standards an elaborate and expensive household was a prerequisite to the married state, but nevertheless a situation which all parties would be glad to end. Morley decided for Dickens; to the sorrow of the pupils and their parents, the school was sold; the move to London was made. In April of 1852 the couple was married in the Unitarian chapel at Newport, Isle of Wight, both families having come round; and a new phase of life began for both.

Journalism was to occupy most of Morley's time for the next fifteen years. During this time his five children grew up around him and in fact mixed with his literary labors. Writing with a baby on his lap, Morley said, was one of his accomplishments. For *Household Words,* much of his work consisted of rewriting contributions sent in by other writers. Dickens was very particular about the polish and tone of his magazine and gave his largely middle- to lower-middle-class readers a considerable bargain at twopence a copy. Among a variety of other topics—the California gold rush, the latest inventions in photography—Morley continued to write on public health, investigating water supplies, burial grounds and epidemics, all matters of concern to Dickens as well as himself.

Morley's versatility as a journalist was aided by his urge to communicate; he really wanted to make a connection with his audience and to interest them in what he had to say. Finding his natural writing style a bit demanding for the readership of *Household Words,* he hit on the advice of the *persona,* writing sometimes as a "gossippy old lady," sometimes as a medical practitioner living in a country village, getting his often somewhat didactic points across while entertaining his readers. From time to time Morley managed to get a piece on literature into *Household Words* or its successor, *All the Year Round*. The following extract from a parody of contemporary book reviews as these appeared in the Victorian press shows Morley's sense of fun and implies as well that Shakespeare's works were a familiar part of even the lower portions of the middle-class world. On the pretense that *"Hamlet*—which, for argument's sake, we will suppose to be a first work—has been distributed with leaves uncut among the critics," Morley gives us first the superficial plot summary, all dashes and exclamations, missing the point of the episodes it describes; then the treatise on the philosophical import of the play's more trivial lines, e.g., "Hail to your lordship!," and finally, most devastating in its blandly condescending tone, a bit of advice:

> We cannot help thinking that the author of this tragedy when he chose Denmark as a scene of action interesting to a reader in this country, might have succeeded better in his purpose had he looked to Iceland for a background to his plot. . . . By the omission of the character of King Claudius the plot would be greatly simplified and the interest of the play would be more strictly centered upon Hamlet. If the work should ever be reprinted (and it certainly has merits which warrant a belief that it may deserve the honors of a second edition), we trust that Mr. Shakespeare will consider it worth while to effect this slight alteration.[5]

Continuing his association as well with Forster's *Examiner*, Morley indulged even more frequently in his preference for writing about literature and the arts. He attended private viewings of the Royal Academy and other art exhibitions, describing the paintings usually in terms of their subjects, a critical perspective he shared with most members of the Victorian public. In his theatre reviews, Morley wrote from a firm appreciation of the cultural importance of the stage, and in this insistence he took a stand which was then more controversial than it has since become. Many of Morley's readers still held the old suspicion of the stage as a haunt of immorality at worst, frivolity at best. In *The Journal of a London Playgoer from 1851 to 1866*, a collection of many of his *Examiner* pieces, Morley points out that London at the time had some twenty or so theaters, several of them quite large (Her Majesty's

Theatre in the Haymarket, for example, then seated 3,000, though it has since been rebuilt on a smaller scale) and that a daily total of 15,000 Londoners attended the theater. His own wish, he says, is "to see our Drama, with a clean tongue and a steady pulse, able to resume its place in society as a chief form of Literature."

As in the other arts, Morley's tastes were close to those of his readers, and he describes elaborate scenery and costumes in tones of satisfaction. He had a protective instinct toward the texts, however. In praising Charles Kean as Shakespeare's Richard II, for instance, he regrets the omission of the scene in Act Five of Aumerle's treachery against Bolingbroke in words which seem intended to encourage his reader to do a little reading on his own: "If we consider the position of each person concerned in the episode, they contain truly the most vigorous sketch ever conceived of the domestic misery that is among the incidents of civil war."

In at least one case, Morley had the experience, probably fairly unusual for a theatre critic, of finding that the recipient of his advice has taken it. Helen Faucit's Lady Macbeth, he felt, was "too demonstrative and noisy" when the production opened; returning a few weeks later, he reported that Miss Faucit, having "like a true actress, profitted from information given from before the curtain," now "avoids all the louder tones in which her voice failed physically to express the thought in her mind, skillfully substituting for them methods of expression perfectly within her range and far more impressive."

From 1856 to 1867 Morley served as editor of *The Examiner*, Forster having resigned to follow other pursuits. For much of this time he had a coeditor to supervise political articles, and he drew on a large number of competent writers as well. Nevertheless, the demand on his time and energy must have been enormous. He was reasonably well paid for his editorship, at a salary of five pounds a week—five shillings less than his *Household Words* salary, which he drew concurrently, holding down in effect two full-time jobs. And this crowded agenda had to be squeezed still further, for it was during this period that Morley returned to the podium as an English teacher.

King's College and the Lecture Circuit

In 1857, the Reverend J. S. Brewer, Professor of English History and Literature at King's College—Morley's alma mater as a medical student—sought a lecturer for two evening classes which he himself had decided, at the last minute, not to take. Morley has met Brewer through his friend James Gairdner of the Public Records Office, who was later to marry Mrs. Morley's younger sister; London's bookish circles formed many interlocking patterns. Although King's College still had its Church of England orientation and Morley as a Unitarian could not have been employed as a regular member of the faculty, the restriction was eased for evening classes, and Morley once again began to teach.

After the wide range of subjects he had covered with his pupils at Liscard, it was perhaps a relief to undertake a narrower endeavor. All Morley had to work up was for Tuesday evenings, "The Origin and Structure of the English Language, Illustrated by Our Literature from the Earliest Times to the Invention of Printing," and, for Friday evenings, "The Principles of Composition, Illustrated by the History of English Literary Composition from the Appearance of Sir Philip Sidney's 'Defence of Poetry' to the Establishment of the *Edinburgh Review.*"[6] (The era encompassed by these two milestones is the seventeenth and eighteenth centuries, with a few additional years on each end.) Henry Shaen Solly, Morley's son-in-law and biographer, who gives us this and other details of the professor's early career in his *Life of Henry Morley,* records Morley's children's memories of their father rushing happily away to his classrooms.

Other evening courses followed; Morley as a lecturer was a definite hit. Speaking without notes and pacing about the platform, he evoked in his listeners the suspicion that if this new subject were all that interesting to the lecturer, then they might find it worth their attention as well. Morley's style was also well suited to his undergraduate audience. His adroit use of facts—lots of facts, with their organizing principles clearly stated—served two purposes. First, of course, they pleased those students whose mental focus was exclusively fixed on their upcoming University of London examinations and who equated a good lecture with a filled notebook; second, the facts fit into the larger patterns of English historical reference which to Morley were becoming increasingly important. His enthusiasm for what he described was genuine; the more he lectured, the more interested he became.

Another reason for Morley's classes' receptive attitude may have been simply the challenge of keeping up with their instructor. Furnivall, who was acquainted with Morley as he was with virtually all of literary London, dropped by his classroom one evening and was struck by the forcefulness of the lecture and the attentiveness of the class, remarking, however, that Morley's "pace was killing." Morley's rejoinder was expressed in his diary; he knew from experience, he said, that a slow and conscientious progress would deaden his listeners much more surely than would a "sharp trot over the ground."[7]

By that point in the nineteenth century, a competent public lecturer, knowledgeable, well able to express himself, and, above all, genuinely eager for his audience to share his pleasure in his subject, would naturally find himself in demand. Word traveled fast. Again and again, from this point in his career until his final years, Morley found himself on a London lecture platform or boarding a train for Birmingham or Leeds, his lecture on the Elizabethan sonneteers or the Arthurian legends in his pocket—from which repository he sometimes neglected to withdraw it, eager as he was to begin and little as he needed his notes. It may be hard for us today to imagine a hall full of people listening attentively to that lore of names and dates, titles and genres, sources and influences, associated today with the drier and more perfunctory phases of the discipline; but, of course, these audiences' school days had lacked that particular asset because it was not available for anybody. It is a curious thing, too, with frameworks, outlines, skeletons of all sorts. One longs to have them, misses them when they are not present, but tends to take them so for granted as soon as they appear, that we today seem to behave as if English literary history just materialized on the ground like manna and never had to be painstakingly worked out.[8]

Morley, however, had no worries about future disregard, and as he planned his courses and gave his lectures, a detailed, systematic history of English literature began to take shape in his mind. His aim was to show how the English character, developing through the ages, is expressed in her literature, which character he saw in a thoroughly Victorian religious light. "The literature of this country has for its most distinctive mark the religious sense of duty. It represents a people striving through successive generations to find out the right and do it," Morley stated in his *First Sketch of English Literature* (1873). In 1864, with the volume just quoted still in the future, Morley found time in his busy schedule to begin this project with the first volume of his *English Writers*. The timing was fortunate. University College had found itself, upon Masson's acceptance of his chair at Edinburgh, in need of an English professor; Morley submitted his name along with a copy of *English Writers*. After the University College governing council had been assured by mutual friends that Morley was an able teacher, he was offered the job and accepted it.

Examinations and Their Discontents

It was a frequent accusation that students at University College, or for that matter students at any of the institutions in the University of London system, were obsessed with examinations to the detriment of their experiencing a genuine liberal arts education.[9] This accusation was to some extent true and is not hard to understand. The students' future lives depended upon examination results to a much greater extent than had been the case in earlier generations, when a smaller and more elite group of young men went to Oxford or Cambridge to broaden their upper middle-class contacts, without usually any great concern about where they stood in their class lists. But in the 1860s, as the various strata of the middle classes expanded and as competition grew along with opportunities, quantitative demonstrations of specific fields of knowledge were emphasized more and more.

From today's perspective—and from the perspective of many observers of the time as well—this focus on examinations brought many disadvantages. A certain grimness, a certain narrowness of outlook and blindness to aspects of the subject at hand which the student saw as unlikely to come up on his examination, irritated professors throughout the century and beyond.

And yet, paradoxically, the situation resulted in part from the Victorians' love of justice. If opportunities were to be given to the most able, then that ability should be measured in an open and visible manner; if, for example, Civil Service jobs in India and elsewhere were to be filled by the best qualified candidates rather than the candidates who happened to know the people who made the decisions, then an examination would produce results against which a charge of favoritism might be harder to make. The consequent danger to the cause of learning through the oversimplification of the subjects taught, and the unhappiness of those candidates whose scores fell just below the acceptance line, were simply the price that had to be paid.

A few additional words might be said in favor of the examination system aside from its alignment with the broader principles of democracy. Competition, after all, can be stimulating as well as terrifying. Dry facts scraped together for an examination may well, in later years or in more interesting contexts, suddenly blossom; should this cheery event occur, one has a basic framework at hand and needn't be forced to begin from scratch. And even the ordeal of putting one's knowledge concisely onto paper, under pressure of time and emotion, can be a salutary one. An examination system, in other words, is certainly not a flawless solution to the problem of evaluating knowledge; but neither should we consider it wholly iniquitous. For the Victorians it represented a new world; education on this scale had never been attempted before, and the details of the process tended to appear in the light more of opportunity than of oppression.

At University College during Morley's time, student life followed the new pattern and began with the University of London's matriculation examination, a hurdle which more or less guaranteed a standard level of preparation in the college classrooms and toward which, the areas covered by these examinations being well publicized, the candidate's past studies might have specifically pointed him. In other words, the subjects set for the examination and the curriculum of many preparatory institutions corresponded closely.

To get into University College, then, according to the official *Calendar*, a student would have to perform satisfactorily in:

1. Latin;
2. *One* of the following languages: Greek, French, German, Sanskrit, Arabic;
3. The English Language; and English History, with the Geography relating thereto;
4. Mathematics;
5. Mechanics;
6. *One* of the following Branches of Science: Chemistry; Heat and Light; Magnetism and Electricity; Botany.

This list gives a good overview of the proportionate ingredients of what was considered by these quite liberal educators a sound college preparation in the later half of the nineteenth century.[10] The emphasis on science is noticeable. ("Mechanics," incidentally, in item (5), refers to "that department of applied mathematics which treats of motion and tendencies to motion," as the *Oxford English Dictionary* explains.) Latin was still essential, and was to remain so for generations, but one

could make a substitution for Greek. No knowledge of English literature as such was required at this point. By "English language" in
item (3) was meant grammar, for the most part.

The above list deals with the subjects a student needed simply to
get into University College. To get out again, with a Bachelor of Arts
granted by the University of London, he needed to survive still another
series of examinations. During Morley's time, the examination for the
B.A. fell into two categories. A student might aim for a "pass" degree,
as most in fact did, or might attempt in addition to take honors in one
of the several areas required for the "pass" degree. This endeavor required additional preparation and yet another examination.

The branches of knowledge dealt with by the "pass" examination
were similar to those listed for the matriculation examination, except
that the specific areas and the various options were considerably more
complex. English was not a required subject for the degree, as it had
been (in the form of grammar) for matriculation. It was, however, one
of a group of language and literature subjects from which the candidate
had to choose one, the others being French, German, Italian, Arabic,
or Sanskrit.

Candidates who chose English for the language and literature requirement of the "pass" degree were then faced with a quite complicated challenge. The English examination would cover three specific
areas: "History, structure, and development of the English Language,"
"Anglo-Saxon Grammar and Translation," and, finally, a list of "Special Subjects" which was changed every year and was announced well
ahead of time, so that a student might prepare in detail. A typical
"Special" list for the "pass" degree, the one announced for the year
1890, near the end of Morley's era and perhaps reflecting his influence
upon it, includes the following:

> History of English Literature from 1625 to 1660
> Shakespeare: *Hamlet*
> Spenser: *The Faerie Queene*, Books I and II
> Dan Michel: *Ayenbite of Inwit*
> Thorpe (ed.): *The Anglo-Saxon Chronicle*, Vol. I.
> Sweet: *Anglo-Saxon Primer*.[11]

The "Thorpe" in the list was Benjamin Thorpe, among the most
prominent Anglo-Saxon scholars of the first half of the century, a student of Rask's and editor of many key texts of the Anglo-Saxon canon,

including *Beowulf*. Henry Sweet's *Anglo-Saxon Primer* had appeared in 1882 as an introduction to the *Anglo-Saxon Reader* compiled by the same formidable scholar and phoneticist. University College was stipulating highly reputable and challenging texts; things were not watered down.

Publishers were as eager to read the lists of books set for the examinations as the candidates were, for they could then brace themselves for an immediate flood of orders. Sometimes the books set for a subject were sold as a unit, done up in a packet. If specific editions were required, students might be given a discount; the Early English Text Society, for example, gave examination candidates a special price. (The examination for the annual E.E.T.S. prize, incidentally, was quite distinct endeavor from the degree examination, being in fact an extracurricular activity.)

The above list, we recall, applies to the "pass' degree only; everyone who chose English as their language option did these preparations. For an honors degree, the candidate prepared all this and more, although, proportionately, the additions are not staggering and usually made a sensible fit with the work already required. For the same year, 1890, subjects sets for the honors examination in English included: History of English Literature from 1660 to 1685; Shakespeare: *The Merchant of Venice*; Bacon: *Essays*; *History of Henry VII*; Cynewulf, *Eléne*.[12] The honors degree in English had been installed at University College in the late 1850s and reflects the growing recognition of the new subject.

Syllabi and Other Specifics

University College offered a three-year course leading to the examinations for the degree, a span of time which was fairly standard for nineteenth-century England. (In Scotland and America the four-year undergraduate course was already the more usual thing, but students in both these countries might well have started younger.) When Morley first took up his duties at University College, English lectures were given to juniors and seniors, second- and third-year men respectively; later, some work in the history and structure of the language was shifted into a course for freshmen. The pattern of a "freshman English" course emphasizing composition had not then been set, and in many colleges on both sides of the Atlantic did not get under way until well into the twentieth century.

Composition was in fact thought of as a fairly advanced type of endeavor, not really suitable for beginners. A student undertaking work in English composition was assumed to have spent some years with Latin rhetoric, classifying the figures of speech and the argumentative strategies. English composition was usually approached by way of precept and example, as may witness the following questions from one of Morley's examinations:

1. Discuss separately the considerations that determine choice and position of words in an English sentence.
2. Describe briefly the argument by which Wordsworth justified the style of his "Lyrical Ballads."
3. Compare, with reference to first principles, the styles of any three important living writers.
4. Write a short essay on the principles of criticism. [13]

To answer these questions the student would have to write an effective composition, so perhaps the focus on principles rather than practice is not really a limiting one. (This examination, by the way, dating from the late 1880s and typical of many others conveniently reproduced in the University College *Calendars*, had nothing to do with the University of London's degree examinations but was simply an internal challenge for Morley's own students.)

Since composition was only one of the things Morley's students did—they spent considerable time as well with early English and with literary history—we might surmise that, even though the *Calendar* described the junior course as including exercises in "the grammatical principles of English composition," the marking of huge batches of weekly themes was not among Morley's sufficiently heavy burden of things to do. This circumstance may go some part of the way toward explaining how he was able to do them all. He constituted for much of his career the entire English Department, though in the 1870s, the College began hiring an assistant for him almost every year.

Morley's chair at that point was not endowed, and his salary depended to a large extent upon his students' fees. Having given up a considerable part of his income when he left journalism, he was naturally pleased to find his classes showing a healthy increase. From a total of 52 juniors and seniors his first year, the number of students in

English courses had doubled by 1873, eight years later; twenty years later, in 1885, the tally reached a high point of 159. Enrollment in University College's Faculty of Arts and Laws, to which the English Department belonged, had risen from 365 to 841 in the meantime.[14]

During these years the content and arrangement of Morley's courses evolved from a rather rigid syllabus for juniors and seniors to a more flexible list of six components, some of them carrying parallel options, which fell under the two heads of language and literature and could be fitted together into a two-year sequence. The material studied remained basically the same, although it benefited from the rearrangement and also from the appearance through the years of improved grammars and other texts, especially in Old and Middle English. In the "language" component of the sequence, students read selections from Sweet's *Anglo-Saxon Reader* and a varying list of Middle English works (*Havelok the Dane*, for example), while attending as well to principles of composition and the history of the language.

Under the various "literature" options, a student could choose one out of two historical periods and could then make another choice among "single works or writers." The content of these options varied from year to year. In 1888, for example, the choices listed in the *Calendar* were:

Periods
    A. The literature from 1558 to 1625, with special studies of Spenser's *Shepheardes Calendar* and of Jonson's masques.
    B. The literature from 1625 to 1685.

Single Works or Writers
    A. Milton's *Comus*, Sonnets, and *Paradise Regained*; Dryden's "Absalom and Achitophel," "The Medal," "The Hind and the Panther"; Browne's *Religio Medici*.
    B. Shakespeare's *King John, Julius Caesar*, and *The Winter's Tale*.[15]

These options in University College's English courses are naturally linked to the special subjects announced for the University of London degree examinations, varying as they did from year to year; we might pause to note some of the advantages of this system. Setting specific subjects ahead of time gave the students an incentive to study the literature in close-up detail, as a change from the more evenly-scaled panorama which the syllabus prescribed as a basis for these special excursions. A practical advantage to the system was, of course, that as the special subjects were changed every year, the students could not profit in too much detail from the experience of their more advanced colleagues. And for the professors teaching the courses which would prepare their students for these examinations, the frequent change must have been refreshing; one could wear out one's tires evenly, so to speak.

Morley, incidentally, served as one of the University of London examiners in English fairly often in his career. (One might be elected to a five-year term, after which one became ineligible for three years but might then be put back on again, and so on.) He was thus responsible in large part for the subjects set and the questions asked about them, a connection which reflects positively on his standing in the profession but which might make his teaching of his own courses potentially suspect. Knowing what the questions would be, he might be tempted to prepare his own students a little too thoroughly. The suspicion is unworthy of us, Morley being in every respect a trustworthy gentleman, but there were some built-in safeguards. Examination questions had to be approved by all the examiners, two to four of them usually to a subject, so that one would have difficulty in proposing a set of questions so eccentric that only one's own students could answer them. Another safeguard existed in the fact that the set subjects were, after all, fairly deep and wide; a professor who dwelt on points that would appear on the exam would have to dwell on a great deal else as well, just for balance.

Morley in the Classroom

To whatever extent they may have been preoccupied by the examinations lurking ahead, Morley's students spent much of their time in the classroom, listening and presumably learning. Here is one of these students, B. Paul Neumann, later a writer of boys' stories, recollecting a typical lecture:

> He [Morley] comes along the corridor from the professors' common room to his classroom. . . . He comes at a good

swinging pace, for the bell has just rung. Under one arm, held akimbo, he carries a huge pile of books, tapering from a folio to a duodecimo. The weight of the pile is considerable, so that he leans heavily on one side. Now he enters the room. . . . After the roll-call, the lecture begins. The lecturer springs to his feet, takes hold of the chair by the back, and, tilting it slightly forward on the front legs, leans over, glancing at an open book or a few brief notes on the table. From these he reads out any necessary dates or facts, often leaving the chair to write them on the blackboard, but generally returning to it before very long. Next comes the clothing and vivifying of the skeleton outline. Without a note he talks on, thoroughly interested himself, and so taking our interest captive, too. Even the chair is abandoned for minutes together, while he walks up and down, his hands locked behind his back, his eyes bright with enthusiasm, misty with quick sympathy, or, oftener still, twinkling with merriment. Now he checks himself in full career to choose some special passage, which he reads out in his own natural but often singularly impressive manner. This is the tit-bit, generally kept to the end, and so liable to be cut short by the importunate bell. Last of all comes a brief levée at the table. Most of those who can, wait behind for a word with the Professor. They thumb his books, make inquiries, pertinent or otherwise, ask advice with reference to their exams, bring up their notes to have lacunae filled up. And he, with a nod and a smile and a cheery word for all, makes everyone welcome, answers every question he can, and if he doesn't know, says so, without any beating around the bush. [16]

Neumann's sketch was written at the request of Solly, who also collected a brief memoir from another former student, "Miss Elsie Day, mistress of Grey Coat School, Westminster":

I first joined what he [Morley] called his "Maidens' Class" in October, 1872. The authorities at University College did not recognize us as students of theirs; we were somehow smuggled in under the wing of a Ladies' Educational Association. Some of the professors looked a little askance at us—we were to be dreaded as an unknown and irregular body—but Professor

Morley neither doubted nor hesitated; he gave us a hearty welcome, and helped us to the uttermost. . . . His old students would all support me in saying that his persistent determination to find something good to say of everyone of whom he spoke was a very marked characteristic of his teaching. Even of so unsavoury a person as Mrs. Aphra Behn he contrived to say some words of deserved praise, bidding us remember her as one of the first to protest against slave traffic. Except in cases of downright meanness or cruelty, he seemed incapable of severity in judgment; not that he called black white, but if, as almost always was the case, white was mixed with the black, it was to the white that our attention was directed.[17]

Morley's preference for accentuating the positive was a genuine part of his nature; it also seems an advantage in dealing with beginners of any sort, since to a beginner his instructor's negative comments are more likely to be taken as a condemnation from on high than as a challenge to further investigation. Independence of judgment appears to be an acquired skill.

The Ladies' Educational Association which conspired to smuggle Miss Day and her classmates under the dome of University College had originated in the north of England in the late 1860s, after which the movement spread over Scotland, England, and parts of the United States. As a transitional measure, these lectures were a diplomatic success, for the ladies at that point were not asking for admission as regular students. They merely borrowed a professor and a classroom, paying a small sum for the privilege, without disturbing in any official way the college or university concerned. In so doing they accustomed themselves to college-level ideas and procedures, and they accustomed the professors to the sight of women in their classrooms. When the University of London opened its degrees to women (with the exception of degrees in medicine) in 1878, many of the basic patterns had already been set.

In the same year, 1878, Morley received another opportunity to support women's education through an appointment to the chair of English at Queen's College, London, an institution founded thirty years earlier by Frederick D. Maurice and several of the latter's colleagues from King's College. Queen's College had taken as its mission the training of governesses; one of its parent bodies was the Governesses' Benevolent Association. Thus the college brought some system and dignity to a calling which had long been a casual and unregulated one. As it happened, the latter half of the nineteenth century saw a decline in private governessing and a rise in teaching opportunities in the emerging British school system. The women of Queen's College thus had access to new realms of professionalism, where the study of English was taking an increasingly important place, and we may assume that Morley found his students attentive and diligent. As it required only a few lectures a week, Morley had no trouble holding the position concurrently with his other duties.

Outside the classroom, Morley supported numerous causes which attempted to enrich student life or simply make that life more comfortable. At University College he founded student clubs and newspapers; he served for a time as principal of a residence hall affiliated with the college; he was instrumental in setting up a tea and refreshment room, the cheerful and convenient descendant of which is still in place. That these amenities should need to be established is an indication not only of the newness of University College but of the bare bones quality of its operating budget; the contrast with life at Oxford or Cambridge, where provisions for recreation and physical comfort were very much a part of the scene, is considerable.

Morley's impulse to add dimensions to his students' lives went beyond the boundaries of College property, and he often invited them to informal Sunday evening gatherings at his home, number eight Upper Park Road in Hampstead. The house, while not palatial, was comfortable and roomy, filled with books, in a neighborhood of trees, hills, and curving streets which has retained much of its charm. Hampstead was then very much a separate village, and the hustle and bustle of London seemed much farther away than it does now. The five children could run about freely and so could the family's pet cat, Boddles, who, on using up the last of his lives after many years of narrow escapes, was buried in the garden beneath a tombstone proudly displaying its scholarly inscription:

REQUIS

CAT

English Writers *and* A First Sketch of English Literature

Morley's ambition to write a definitive English literary history was frustrated first because he had so many things to do besides write, and second because the writing he did do—an astonishing lot of it—tended to fulfill his public's demands rather than to follow his own preferences. In a sense, he was too popular for his own good.

Volume one of *English Writers*, which we last saw in 1865, was for almost two decades alone on its shelf, awaiting the remainder of what Morley projected as a twenty-volume work. In 1873, however, Morley published his *First Sketch of English Literature*, incorporating some material from his earlier volume but taking the story into the nineteenth century. For the 1886 edition, Morley added a lengthy chapter, "Of English Literature in the Reign of Victoria," describing the work of Dickens, Thackeray, and other contemporaries, and bringing the picture very much up-to-date. From its title, A *First Sketch* sounds like a bare pamphlet, but it ran in its later editions to some thousand pages. It also became very popular, selling some 30,000 copies and making more money for the author than any of his other books.

Morley's writing style is that of the brisk classroom lecturer, out to catch his hearers' attention and then lead them on to the main points. "Once Europe was peopled only here and there by men who beat at the doors of nature and upon the heads of one another with sharp flints," he writes in his opening pages, and goes on to weave together literary events with their historical reference points. "Bede, born in 673, was a child in arms when Caedmon sang the power of the Creator and his counsel, and young Aldhelm had begun his work at Malmesbury. When seven years old—that is to say, about the time of the death of Abbess Hilda—Bede was placed in the newly-founded monastery of St. Peter, at Wearmouth."[18]

Morley may have seen the success of A *First Sketch* as more or less accidental, the consequence of its managing to get itself finished. His heart was in *English Writers*. The series got under way again in the 1880s, picked up considerable speed upon Morley's retirement from teaching in 1889, and by his death in 1894 had arrived not at its destination but halfway. Of his projected twenty volumes, ten had been published and the eleventh was in preparation.

Here Morley's focus is minute. Volume two brings the story only up to the Norman conquest; volume three, to Chaucer, and volume four, through the fourteenth century. By volume eight, having moved on to the Renaissance, Morley covers the ground from Surrey up to Spenser, while volume nine is devoted almost entirely to Spenser. Volume ten, published in 1893, brings Shakespeare through the reign of Queen Elizabeth; volume eleven, prepared by one of Morley's former students, W. Hall Griffin, with the addition of a chapter of his own and a bibliography, brings the coverage of Shakespeare to completion in 1616.

One suspects that the readers of these volumes found themselves longing for the old sharp trot over the ground. The pace is slow, the summaries of literary works interminable—forty pages on King Alfred, five on Roger Ascham's *The Schoolmaster*. In all, *English Writers* could hardly be said to have become the achievement Morley had in mind. The text is simply too cumbersome to demonstrate a unified view of the English national character; the reader gets lost in the detail, volume after volume, excursion after excursion. Luckily, since he was so heartily occupied during his final years with putting the series together, Morley may not have realized its ultimate failure to thrive.

Editions of the Classics

In the meantime, throughout most of his professorial career Morley had supplied his several publishers with brief, factual introductions to the low-priced reprints of "literary classics" offered to a public increasingly eager to build up their home libraries. (The word "classic" was beginning to lose its connotation of Greek and Roman literature exclusively and to take on, at least to the general public, a connotation of tradition and respectability. Its application to English literature could be seen as an indication of the increased esteem in which the products of the native tongue were held.) These sets of books, often called "libraries," were usually issued one volume at a time, at regular intervals, and were purchased either by a prearrangement to subscribe to the entire lot (in which case the buyer received a discount) or separately, volume by volume.

Sets with which Morley had something to do include an enterprise named for him, *Morley's Universal Library*, published by G. Routledge and Sons and comprised of rather miscellaneous reprints, ranging from More's *Utopia* to translations of Spanish ballads; *Cassell's Library of English Literature*, an anthology in five volumes, one of which (the third, *English Plays*) provided the only collection of non-Shakespearean early drama within reach of student budgets in the 1870s and was used as a textbook in the United States as well as in England; the *Carisbrooke Library*, published by G. Routledge and Sons; and *Cassell's National Library*, probably Morley's most influential editorial labor since there was so much of it.

Morley's biographer Solly describes the genesis and the success of the latter series, of which several hundred titles (most but not all edited by Morley) eventually appeared and in many cases reappeared, the reprints continuing well into the twentieth century:

> [A]n article in the *Daily News* in the summer of 1885, calling attention to the fact that we have nothing in England corresponding to the famous threepenny series in Germany, promptly produced a request from Cassell and Company that Professor Morley would undertake to edit such a series. He accepted their proposals, and Cassell's "National Library" was the result. Here the issue was in weekly volumes, and continued for about five years. At a cost not exceeding the gas or water rate, a constant supply of good literature could be "laid on" to any house in town or country, and a circulation varying from 50,000 to 100,000 copies for each volume attests the popular appreciation of the enterprise. Letters, which Professor Morley greatly prized, came from the far West in America, and from other lands on the borders of civilization, expressing gratitude for these cheap and handy volumes.[19]

This great flood of books—each volume small in size, about four-by-six inches, containing about two hundred pages and costing sixpence in a paper cover or a shilling in a cloth one—testifies to the eagerness with which the general public tried to make good literature a part of their lives. Some part of the purchaser's impulse may have come from snobbery, or perhaps from good intentions never fulfilled; but many volumes surely were read, and one pictures a family gathered around the lamplight in a lonely homestead on the American plains, reading aloud, caught up perhaps in *Tintern Abbey* or the essays of Bacon. (Solly, to whom such outposts seemed as remote as another planet, might have added to this vision the howling of wolves on the horizon; but perhaps we are being melodramatic.) The success of this venture testifies as well to the extent to which education was spreading through the orders of society. School systems in England, the United States, and Canada and Australia (where, Solly observes at another point, Morley's low-cost editions were much favored) were teaching people not only to read but to value what they could read. It is useful to keep in mind that the growth of English studies in the universities was sustained from beneath, so to speak, by this increasing popular awareness of their value.

The dozen or so Shakespeare plays included in *Cassell's National Library* seem to have been particularly close to Morley's heart. The texts were carefully chosen and edited, that of *Hamlet*, for example, as Morley tells us, "freshly compared throughout with the texts of the first and second quarto and of the First Folio." The introductions to the volumes, two-to-four pages in length, consisted largely of factual information—historical connections, sources of the plots, and so on. There were no textual notes, a disadvantage which would seem a crippling one for an inexperienced reader of Shakespeare. Presumably the addition of such notes would have made the volumes too expensive, and they then could not have been published at all. Morley, quite sensitive to the difficulty, proposes a rather wistful solution: "If life and health suffice to the completion of the plan here sketched, the series of the plays will be followed by three or four volumes of selected and original Notes." Morley's life and health stretched to encompass a great many literary undertakings, but, unfortunately, not this one.

Last Years

In his seventies, retired to the Isle of Wight, surrounded by his affectionate friends and family and saddened only by the death of his wife two years before his own, Morley could look back on a life filled with satisfactions.

Among his permanent accomplishments were his books, or so it must have seemed, for they existed in solid three-dimensional form on his own and many other library shelves; the ruinous passage of time and fashion is not the sort of thing a writer with a basically happy disposition thinks about. These writings were considerably more voluminous than the total of those mentioned here would indicate. Apart from his journalistic work, Morley in his earlier years had published a series of biographies of historical figures, several volumes of fairy tales— many of them springing from his pleasure in inventing stories for his own children—and even, during his early days as a medical practitioner with an occasional spare moment for literature, a slim volume of poetry entitled *The Dream of the Lilybell*.

Morley's former students must also have been a permanent and tangible satisfaction. Of the thousands who sat in his classrooms or attended his special lectures, two might have special mention. Edward Arber had been one of Morley's evening students at King's College in the late 1850s; after an initial career in the Civil Service, he changed direction and became Morley's assistant at University College between 1879 and 1881. From there he went on, as Professor of English, to Mason College in Birmingham, a newly founded institution later to become part of the University of Birmingham. Arber's interests in English Renaissance literature led him to transcribe and edit the *Registers of the Company of Stationers, 1554–1640*, still a standard work.

Walter Raleigh (not the earlier notable of that name) studied with Morley in the late 1870s and went on to take an undergraduate degree at Cambridge. In 1889 he became Professor of English at the University of Liverpool and in 1904, ten years after Morley's death, he accepted the new chair of English literature at Oxford and there enjoyed a distinguished career.

Less tangible yet of great value was the service Morley performed to the discipline of English language and literature. His efforts took the subject far along the road to respectability. He managed to combine two roles, that of the popularizer—the platform lecturer, the editor of mass-produced classics—and of the intellectual father-figure, learned and minute. In this last regard we might remind ourselves once again that the details of literary history so easily accessible today were then being discovered and joined together, and the body of knowledge acquired by the participants in this enterprise was accorded sincere respect. Morley thus embodied the Victorian ideal of the trustworthy reformer, the man whose ideas, however untraditional at first glance, will nevertheless turn out to be sound. If Morley said English language and literature was an important study, the Victorians were willing to listen. David J. Palmer, tracing the new subject from the seventeenth century to the establishment of the English School at Oxford (*The Rise of English Studies*, Oxford University Press, 1965), devotes three pages of his brisk narrative to a summary of Morley's accomplishments and includes this tribute:

> To Henry Morley belongs the distinction of being the first to devote an academic career solely to English studies, if we except Masson, whose last thirty years were spent in Scotland. For nearly forty years Morley held university posts connected with the teaching of English literature; with him English studies become fully professional, and by the end of his career we are almost in the modern period. [20]

3

Francis James Child (1825–1896), Harvard, and *The English and Scottish Popular Ballads*

In America, where innovation stood a greater chance against tradition simply because there was less tradition, the study of English slipped into higher education without major upheavals of the sort faced in many British institutions. This process may have been helped by the fact that English literature was associated with the faraway homeland and consequently may have been more cherished, less taken for granted; it gained an automatic nostalgia value.

That America's openness to English studies did not constitute an opposition to the ancient languages can be seen in the universal assumption that the classics formed a necessary foundation for higher learning. In Boston, the importance of Latin as a college prerequisite served as a social dividing line; students who planned to go to college attended the Boston Latin School while those who did not attended the English High School. Francis James Child was a product of both, having graduated from the English High School with such distinction that he was urged by the headmaster of the Latin School, Epes Sargent Dixwell, to prepare himself for college. Tradition says that Dixwell backed up his encouragement with a loan, which Child repaid as soon as he could.[1]

Child thus rose from the Boston working class into which he was born to a secure professional niche. His father was a sailmaker, an occupation which seems at least in retrospect quite a romantic one. James Donald Reppert in his Harvard dissertation, *F. J. Child and the Ballad* (1953), suggests alternate visions of Child's boyhood:

> It is a question whether we are to imagine him lingering along the wharves absorbing a tradition of sea-song and wonder-

65

telling or whether we are to see him (at the kitchen table?) poring over the favored intricacies of rhetoric, mathematics, and grammar. Results seem to favor the latter.[2]

There is no reason Child could not have managed both the sea chanties and the homework, but whatever the circumstances may have been, Child appears to have left the scenes of his early life quite definitively behind when he entered Harvard in the fall of 1842. His life thereafter was centered in Cambridge, geographically only a few miles from Boston but culturally another case entirely, from the standpoint at least of its inhabitants. And Boston, during Child's lifetime, altered itself so remarkably that Child may have felt after a few decades that his boyhood belonged to a long-ago era. When Child was born in 1825, the Back Bay was literally a bay, full of water, the city's original harbor, and Boston Common was on the shoreline. (Longfellow's poem on the midnight ride of Paul Revere follows this earlier topography.) The reclamation of the Back Bay, which increased the city's size by a thousand acres and gave it what then became its most exclusive residential area, took place between 1856 and 1886. Streets were straightened and widened, public gardens laid out, pilings set into the reclaimed but still soggy ground for the buildings which were then erected on them. The coming of the railways in the 1840s, and a major fire in the 1870s, had their effects on the changing cityscape. Steamships had begun to crowd out the sailing vessels at the new wharves, and Child would have had difficulty in following his father's occupational footsteps even if he had wanted to.

Harvard in the Nineteenth Century

Cambridge escaped this fervor and remained a quiet village, its focus Harvard Yard, its modest but comfortable residences interspersed by orchards, vegetable gardens, and cow pastures. Harvard Yard was not only quiet but dark; in the 1840s gas lighting had not yet been installed, either indoors or out, and Child and his classmates could conveniently indulge in nocturnal wanderings from building to building only on moonlit nights. If there was no moon, they were expected to spend their evenings in one place, preferably in their rooms and at their desks. These rooms were at least warm, or capable of being made warm, since a student was charged $6.50 per ton for wood, or $7 per ton for coal. The college catalogues did not specify the amount of fuel a student might expect to use for heating his room, but total expenses for tuition, room, board and textbooks were estimated at $194 for the year, comprising two terms. These figures were to rise somewhat during the century. In terms of buying power the sums were substantial (one could buy a reasonably good horse, for example, for ten dollars) and if it is true that Child's Harvard career was made possible by headmaster Dixwell, the latter performed an act of considerable generosity.

As an undergraduate in the early 1840s, Child underwent an education which stressed not only the classical languages and literatures but rhetoric and declamation, both traditional humanist disciplines. At this point freshmen had no elective subjects and divided their time among courses in Greek, Latin, mathematics, and history (the history, that is, of ancient Greece and Rome). In the sophomore year rhetoric was required, and there was some choice in the continuing study of mathematics, Greek, or Latin. Sophomores might also begin a modern language. Rhetoric continued as a requirement for both the junior and senior years, with the additional possibility of continuing any of the subjects begun earlier or of starting some new electives—botany, mineralogy, geology.

A closer view of what all that rhetoric meant in terms of the students' coursework is provided by the *President's Report* of 1845–46, which explains of the Department of Rhetoric and Oratory, headed by Edward T. Channing, Boylston Professor of Rhetoric and Oratory, that:

> Instruction in this Department is given to the three upper classes, by Exercises in Reading, Speaking, and Composition, by Recitations in Grammar, Rhetoric, and Logic, and by Lectures.
>
> The Sophomores recited three times a week from Lowth's Grammar, and Campbell's Rhetoric, during the first term.
>
> One half presented Themes and attended a critical exercise upon them, every week, during the year. [This statement seems to mean that each sophomore wrote a theme every two weeks.]
>
> To the Juniors instruction was given by Exercises in Composition and Speaking, and by Recitations, three times a week during the second term, from Whately's Logic.

They presented Themes, and attended a critical exercise upon them, once a fortnight, during the year.

They declaimed, by sections of nine, every week.

To the Seniors instruction was given by Exercises in Composition and Speaking, which occupied a like time, and were conducted in the same manner, as those of the Juniors. They also attended recitations from Whately's Rhetoric, or public lectures on Rhetoric, twice a week during the first term.

Each Sophomore presented sixteen themes, each Junior sixteen, each Senior sixteen.[3]

Harvard graduates of that era, for example the author of *The Education of Henry Adams,* credit their college experiences with ridding them forever of self-consciousness in speaking before an audience.

In the "recitation" system used in the courses described above, the instructor asked a question and the student, to show he had properly prepared the assignment, answered it. The lecture, in which the instructor spoke and the student took notes, was to constitute a later development at Harvard, although it was already in use in many parts of England and was a favored method in the German universities. In Child's day the recitation method had become something of a totalitarian mechanism. Kermit Vanderbilt, in his biography of Child's friend and classmate Charles Eliot Norton, gives an impression of it:

> The recitation method gave to many a classroom the fearsome atmosphere of a police station. Teachers were not expected to inspire the student, but to cross-examine him on his prepared lessons. . . . The "Scale of Merit" was geared to the recitation method. It granted a daily eight points toward graduation honors to the student who had recited his lessons properly. But deductions for unprepared lessons or for slips in discipline could wipe out several days of merit points. Sixteen credits were subtracted for skipping Sunday chapel, and thirty-two for failure to prepare a theme or declamation.[4]

Vanderbilt goes on to point out that some instructors refused to conduct their classes on this system, among them the poet Henry Wadsworth Longfellow, at that time Harvard's Professor of Belles Lettres.

The recitation method, so condescending to the student as to seem to undermine today's ideas of the first principles of a liberal education, might possibly have had some advantages, though not enough, probably, for anyone to want to bring it back. It might, for example, inculcate regular and matter-of-fact work habits. It may also have simplified the social relationships between members of the classes. Performances were so public, and the rewards and punishments so simple; one could follow one's own progress and one's classmates' quite easily, since a student either knew the answer when called upon or didn't; one could keep score oneself, if one liked, without seeming unduly obsessed about it. In fact, in view of the boredom which doubtless accompanied an hour of questions and answers in the alphabetical order of the roll call, round and round the room, keeping score was perhaps the only way to keep from falling over. From the standpoint of getting along with one's peers, the passivity of the student in this exchange may have been a useful circumstance. No one had to volunteer, to thrust his knowledge forward or seek attention; one could be remarkably modest and remarkably successful, simultaneously.

This situation may have been helpful to Child. He was without family connections, wealth, or any of the usual boosts to status in an adolescent culture. Physically he was not prepossessing—fine boned, with curly hair and a round face, already known by the nickname he retained all his life of "Stubby." And he was, inevitably, tops in every class. Mathematics, history, Latin, or Greek—the instructor questioned and Child answered. His classmates are on record as saying they didn't mind it. The memoirs collected after his death may of course have been altered in the minds of the writers by Child's later recognition, so that he became a desirable acquaintance in retrospect; but enough voices chime in describing Child's unpretentious friendliness, his sense of humor, and his passion for scholarship to suggest some truth in the picture. He read books on his own, followed his own curiosity in its own directions. He developed a learned, judicious writing style. It would seem almost as if he had taken on at the age of seventeen the professorial role he would play for the rest of his life. But it was, clearly, very much what he wanted. And he had done it all himself.

Child Joins the Faculty

On completing his undergraduate career with distinction, having been chosen class orator, and having won a Bowdoin Prize for an essay on

"The Moral Views of Plato as Unfolded in the Gorgias,'" Child was immediately offered an instructorship at Harvard. In view of his literary interests, which had taken precedence over his other subjects although he continued to receive excellent marks in everything, it may seem odd that the instructorship was in mathematics. A narrow concept of specialization was not typical of the times, however. College instructors were versatile beings.

Harvard clearly wanted to do its best to match Child's preferences to the work they could give him, for the catalogues' faculty lists for the period show a continual edging over into greener pastures. By 1849, mathematics left behind, Child appears as "Tutor in History and Political Economy, and Instructor in Elocution." (The word "tutor" did not carry the connotation it did in the older British universities, that of someone who supervised all the studies of a specific group of students. Like "instructor," the word simply meant a fairly low-ranking member of an academic department.) Elocution, as we have noticed, was closely linked to the study of rhetoric and thus to the ancestral form of the English Department as it evolved at Harvard and in many other places.

An effective way of indicating to one's university the direction in which one's scholarly interest lies is to publish something in that area, and this Child rather quickly did, becoming an editor of English drama. In 1848 his *Four Old Plays* was published by George Nichols and Company of Cambridge and was well received as a competent scholarly production. These plays dated from the sixteenth century and consisted of the anonymous "Thersytes" and "Jack Juggler," John Heywood's "The Pardoner and the Friar," all short pieces in the interlude tradition, and a longer tragedy, *Jocasta*, adapted from Euripides by Francis Kinwelmarsh and George Gascoigne. Child edited the texts from a printed source of considerable rarity—one of thirty-five copies printed in 1820 for the Roxburghe Club, one of the most elite of the British "printing societies." By choosing this collection of plays, Child did more than make the texts more easily available. Through his editorial and critical apparatus, he put the plays into a useful context from the standpoint both of literary history and of philology.

This early work is overshadowed by Child's later achievements with the popular ballads and is seldom mentioned in accounts of his career, but it gives some interesting indications of Child's way of going about things. Introduction, notes, and glossary are thorough and sound.

Each of the plays is related to its antecedents in Greek or Roman literature and is also discussed in terms of its themes as treated in other English works; Child comments, for example, on Dryden's later treatment of the Alcmena story in Plautus's *Amphitryon*, the source of the anonymous "Jack Juggler." The sense of literature as embracing many countries, languages, and historial periods is everywhere in Child's commentaries, foreshadowing the sensibility he was later to bring to his studies of the ballads. Another of Child's basic attitudes, later to reappear frequently, had to do with the nineteenth-century public's scruples as to less than refined language. Here Child announced his determination to adhere to the originals in their complete and accurate forms. "The indelicacies of language, which are somewhat frequent in these interludes, never amounting to immoralities, though sufficiently gross, have not been considered of such a nature as to justify a mutilation of the text,"⁵ he states firmly. Finally, since the edition retains the sixteenth-century spelling and punctuation, both notes and glossary demonstrate Child's extensive knowledge of the earlier forms of the English language, a knowledge he had acquired on his own in what spare time he could find.

Whether or not in direct response to the appearance of *Four Old Plays*, Harvard in 1849 provided Child with a leave of absence enabling him to go abroad for further studies. For a scholar with philological leanings in the mid-nineteenth century, there was only one destination.

On to Germany

Berlin was then the capital of the Kingdom of Prussia, though at the time of Child's visit the city had not yet undergone the boom in prosperity and population that followed the winning of the Franco-Prussian war (1870–71). It was then smaller and sleepier, with narrow cobbled streets and three-story houses. The University, however, was extraordinarily alive. It had been founded only in 1810, upon Prussia's loss of the University of Halle; Napoleon had annexed the latter city in his newly created kingdom of Westphalia, a circumstance which may serve to remind us of the constantly shifting political boundaries within the area we are simply denoting as Germany.

The University of Berlin differed from Harvard in ways which Child must have found exhilerating. Academic life was on a much larger scale. There was more of everything—more scholars, more lectures, more books old and new, more awareness of the latest advances of knowledge in a wide variety of fields. And into all of this foreign visitors were welcome to plunge. (The ability to speak and read German was, of course, fairly essential to full enjoyment; but this prerequisite seemed to give Child no trouble, as languages came easily to him.) One could attend lectures without having matriculated for a specific degree, and the state of Prussia, which maintained and supervised the universities, had taken several steps to ensure the depth and variety of lectures available. Full professors, for example, were required to give a certain number of free lectures in their subject—as many, in some cases, as two a week. Thus any student who felt a sudden impulse toward a subject had no difficulty in following it up. Further enrichment of the lecture scene came from the institution of the *privatdocent*, a peculiarly German arrangement in which a sort of assistant professor, approved by the university to which he was attached but not salaried, might give lectures and charge fees for them. Matthew Arnold, whose endorsement of the German system was enthusiastic, describes this state of things from the perspective of the 1880s:

> In general, as I have said, the professors and *Privatdocenten* arrange together to parcel out the field of instruction between them, and one supplements the other's teaching; still a *Privatdocent* may, if he likes, lecture on just the same subject that a professor is lecturing on; there is absolute liberty in this respect. The one precaution taken against undue competition is, that a *Privatdocent* lecturing on a professor's subject is not allowed to charge lower fees than the professor. It does honor to the disinterested spirit in which science is pursued in Germany, that with these temptations to competition the relations between the professors and the *Privatdocenten* are in general excellent. . . . But it is evident how the neighborhood of a rising young *Privatdocent* must tend to keep a professor up to the mark, and hinder him from getting sleepy and lazy. If he gets sleepy and lazy, his lecture room is deserted. The *Privatdocent*, again, has the standard of eminent men under his eyes, and everything stimulates him to come up to it.[6]

This example of a free and constructive sharing between old and young scholars in a common academic pursuit may have served as a model for Child's later generous relationships with his own students. In Germany, too, professors were encouraged to teach subjects simply because they thought them worth doing, even if the general public or the student body had never heard of them; and such an atmosphere may have helped Child to develop his own initiative in this regard. For some years thereafter, the lectures in English which Child gave at Harvard were more his idea than the authorities', and Child had to invest a great deal of his own energy in the project before results were apparent.

At Berlin, Child came under the influence of the great Jacob Grimm, whose linguistic theories had begun startling the world only a few decades previously, and of Grimm's various followers (including, we might surmise, a few intense young *privatdocenten*). While Grimm's theories of language were of special interest to Child in their bearings on Anglo-Saxon and early English, the view held by Grimm of world literature as an interconnected pattern was also to form the basis of Child's work in the ballads. Several ballads of which only puzzling fragments can be found in English are illuminated by Child's knowledge of their counterparts in German or Danish.

Moving on to the University of Göttingen, in the Electorate of Hanover, Child found himself at a somewhat older university (though in fact younger than Harvard) with a historical connection to England; it had been founded in the 1730s by King George II, a Hanoverian. Here Child worked under two eminent philologists of the day, Friedrich Wilhelm Schneidewinn and Karl Friedrich Hermann, and began the preparation of a doctoral thesis which he did not complete. George Lyman Kittredge, a later student of Child's and the author of several biographical sketches of his mentor, suggests that the completion of the thesis would have narrowed Child's pursuits at a time when he wanted to be more free to explore. In any case, his work and his abilities must have impressed the authorities at Göttingen, for in 1853, after Child had returned to Harvard, they surprised and delighted him by granting him an honorary Ph.D. Honorary degrees were not given lightly in those days; Child happily claimed his, and it appears after his name in the official faculty lists thereafter. This circumstance has caused some biographical confusion, and Child is sometimes said to have remained at Göttingen until 1853 when he came home with the degree. The error is perhaps understandable because acquiring a doctorate in Ger-

many was a frequent American undertaking and also because the year
or so which Child spent in his studies abroad seems so short a time.
He must have felt quite conscious of the need to get the most from his
experiences. Kittredge felt no doubt but that he profited from them:

> In the three or four decades preceding Mr. Child's residence
> in Europe, Germanic philology (in the wider sense) had
> passed from the stage of "romantic" dilettantism into the con-
> dition of a well organized and strenuous scientific discipline,
> but the freshness and vivacity of the first half of the century
> had not vanished. Scholars, however severe, looked through
> the form and strove to comprehend the spirit. The ideals of
> erudition and of a large humanity were not even suspected
> of incompatibility. The imagination was still invoked as the
> guide and illuminator of learning. The bond between an-
> tiquity and medievalism and between the Middle Ages and
> our own century was never lost from sight. It was certainly
> fortunate for American scholarship that at precisely this junc-
> ture a young man of Mr. Child's ardent love of learning,
> strong individuality, and broad intellectual sympathies was
> brought into close contact with all that was most quickening
> in German university life. He attended lectures on classical
> antiquity and philosophy, as well as on Germanic philology;
> but it was not so much by direct instruction that he profited
> as by the inspiration which he derived from the spirit and the
> ideals of foreign scholars, young and old. His own greatest
> contribution to learning, *The English and Scottish Popular
> Ballads*, may even, in a very real sense, be regarded as the
> fruit of those years in Germany.[7]

Child Becomes Professor of Rhetoric

In 1851 Child returned to Harvard to take up a new set of duties as
Boylston Professor of Rhetoric and Oratory, upon the retirement of
Professor Channing, previous holder of the chair. Child thus undertook
a twenty-five year stint of marking student themes, a chore which he
performed conscientiously but did not like. Toward the end of this
period, he did receive some assistance in the form of an Assistant

Professor in Rhetoric. In the meantime, however, there was a great deal to do, most of it more congenial than theme marking, as Child introduced more and more English literature into the curriculum.

Unlike most English universities and like most American ones, Harvard did not grant its degrees upon the student's passing one ultimate set of examinations. Instead, the student passed his courses one at a time, or four or so at a time rather, and was given his degree upon his completing a sufficient number of them, as is the case today. A course was defined by the catalogue as "a single line of study receiving three hours a week of instruction," boundaries which also sound familiar to students today. As late as the 1880s, a passing grade in a course was fifty percent of the maximum—a tabulation which has been altered.

The increasing introduction of elective subjects at Harvard, which system percolated from senior to freshman level during the second half of the nineteenth century, appears to have a direct bearing upon the expansion of course offerings in English. By the end of Child's career, the English Department not only had come into being but was flourishing with a large faculty and many courses. During the 1850s, however, when development of the new subject was carried on under the flag of rhetoric and when the elective system was taking a tentative kind of root (the first students faced with the prospect of choosing some of their own courses were urged to seek the advice not only of their parents and their professors but also of any college graduates they happened to know), change came slowly.

Immediately upon returning from Germany, and without waiting for the tide of electives to reach his discipline, Child began to put English studies into his teaching whenever he could. "The Gothic and Anglo-Saxon languages are taught (to those who desire to learn them), by Professor Child," notes the *Catalogue* of 1852–53. The success of this effort, a voluntary one on the part of both students and instructors, is not recorded, but apparently undergraduates were found capable of learning Anglo-Saxon; for that language was added to the required sophomore course in rhetoric in 1854. Rhetoric also expanded its boundaries in the senior course, when students were assigned, in addition to their themes and declamations, a weekly lecture (Mondays at noon in Harvard Hall) on English language and literature. Over the next few decades, these new components were shifted about in the rhetoric program. In the early 1860s, for example, sophomores studied

Anglo-Saxon during the first term and "readings in English literature" during the second.

In the middle and late 1860s, electives for the junior and senior classes expanded to include, for juniors, a course given by Child in "The English Language," comprising Anglo-Saxon and Middle English readings, the Bible, Spenser, and Shakespeare. By 1869 this course emphasized Chaucer's *Prologue* to the *Canterbury Tales*, and the *Knight's Tale*. Seniors also might elect an intensive course in Anglo-Saxon, building presumably on the exposure they had had earlier in the required rhetoric course.

English literature also plays a prominent if extracurricular role in several of the competitions which enlivened undergraduate life. The Bowdoin Prize, the Boyleston Prize, and two exhibitions in the art of reading aloud deserve special notice.

The Bowdoin Prize, one of which Child had captured as an undergraduate, might more accurately have been called the Bowdoin Prizes, since they existed in numerous categories and gradations. Juniors, seniors, and graduate students could enter, competing in their respective lists for prizes ranging from fifteen to forty dollars—weighty sums in those days. Specific topics were set each year and included not only essays written in English but translations from English into Latin or Greek prose or poetry. A typical challenge was that of putting a passage from Pope's "Essay on Man" into Latin hexameters. If they wished to submit an essay written in English, contestants could choose from two or three possibilities each year, usually including ancient history and political science; but English literature made increasingly frequent appearances as Child settled into his chair. "A History and Criticism of the Text of Shakespeare's Plays," "Shakespeare's and the Greek Tragedians' Portraits of Women," and "A Sketch of the History of English Religious Poetry from the Beginning of the Sixteenth Century" are a few examples.[8] These papers were to be researched and written by the student on his own, assisted only incidentally by any lectures he might have been attending, although one assumes that in the case of an English literature paper some suggestions and encouragement might have been available from the Professor of Rhetoric.

Competition for the Boyleston Prize for Elocution, which involved Child's duties quite directly, took place as a public entertainment on the day after graduation exercises in July. Sophomores through seniors (graduated seniors, that is, of the previous day) might take part, having chosen and prepared "pieces in prose or verse from English, Greek, or Latin authors, the selection to be approved by the Boyleston Professor of Rhetoric and Oratory."[9] Of the pieces chosen, the proportion in English was required to be two out of three at least—a stipulation which presumably allowed the audience to feel more a part of things. Several hours of Latin orations on a July day might have led to restlessness. Pieces were to be memorized, and memorized well: "At this exhibition, no prompting of the speakers will be allowed, and a failure of memory in anyone will exclude him from being considered in the assignment of prizes."[10] Judges were imported from the outside world, "five gentlemen distinguished for their elocution, either at the bar, in the pulpit, or in the senate,"[11] and one cannot help wondering if this array of authority, together with the presence in the audience of family and sweethearts, and the dire consequence of a lapse of memory, ever rendered a candidate speechless in mid-strophe. Prizes were gold medals of a value from ten to fifteen dollars. The criteria upon which Child was expected to approve or disapprove the candidates' oratorical selections are not stipulated in the *Catalogue*.

Finally, Harvard encouraged skill in reading aloud, a valued accomplishment in the days before family entertainment could be obtained from a television set, and an indication of culture and taste as well. The competition, in which winners received up to twenty dollars' worth of books, stressed quick preparation and also reflects Child's preference, noted by several of his former students, for low-key and expressive reading over a more formulaic or prefabricated style of oratory. Here the candidates had no choice of script; "The pieces to be read will be placed in the hands of the candidates on the morning of the day of trial. In their selection, declamatory pieces will be avoided, and such narratives, descriptions, or essays chosen as shall require varied expression and correct enunciation."[12] Earlier practice in this art was available to freshmen, who were required to do some reading aloud as part of Harvard's quite strenuous entrance examination. The purpose here may have been to spot promising elocutionists, or simply to find out if an aspiring freshman could read at all, or perhaps both. Candidates prepared from a list announced well in advance; in 1870, for instance, one could choose a selection from either *Julius Caesar* or *Comus*—and, having been admitted on the strength of a passable job, could then compete for a small prize offered freshmen for an excellent one.

While discharging his varied duties as Professor of Rhetoric, Child made room in his life for marriage and a family, marrying in 1860 Elizabeth Ellery Sedgwick, of the New York Sedgwicks. This marriage is perhaps an indication of the extent to which Child had by that time built a world for himself in the intellectual circles of Cambridge. With his scholarly achievements and with the respect he had gained as a man of integrity as well as of ability, he appears to have taken his place as head of his household quite self-confidently, undismayed by in-laws who frequented Newport and took luxurious trips to Europe. With their four children the Childs lived within easy walking distance of Harvard Yard, in a comfortable house at 67 Kirkland Street, where the large front lawn was given over to the Professor's rose garden. Here Child balanced his scholarly efforts with hours given to his family, his roses, and politics both local and national; like most of his colleagues, he was strongly pro-Union during the American Civil War of 1861–65.

The English Courses Take Root

Harvard's first chair of English, as distinct from Rhetoric, was established in 1876, and Child at the age of fifty-one was the obvious person to fill it. Child's assistant in the teaching of rhetoric, Adams Sherman Hill, became Boylston Professor.

Child then found himself teaching four elective courses in English. These included two courses in Anglo-Saxon, the second of which included *Beowulf;* a literature course emphasizing Chaucer, Bacon, Milton, and Dryden; and finally the Shakespeare course, Child's most popular offering and the one with which he seems to have left a permanent impression upon the undergraduate memory of the period. This course consisted of a close reading of some eight or ten of Shakespeare's plays and was so set up, by alternating the works studied, that a student might take it twice without repeating the assignments. (Harvard students who studied Shakespeare with Kittredge, Child's successor, will perhaps recognize the pattern of close textual study.)

Child in the classroom seems to have left varied impressions. Certainly he demanded hard work. An anonymous memoir published in the Boston *Transcript* shortly after Child's death gives a picture of the professor at work, from a viewpoint sympathetic to the ordinary student:

No one who ever saw or talked with Professor Child could forget the intellectual vigor of the man or his quaint personality. Very short of stature, his large head covered with thick, curly hair seemed the greater part of his body, his short sighted eyes gleamed brilliantly behind his spectacles, and lost nothing which came within their limited range. In his courses in Shakespeare and Chaucer he became renowned for his self-absorption, and being first of all a scholar, talked and lectured more to himself than to his students. . . . Professor Child was by nature an extremely dogmatic man, and would not brook an attempt to controvert his own judgment unless there was a good substantial reason for it. With the Baconian theory he had no patience, and would have little to say in favor of the extravagant opinion of Shakespeare commentators which naturally come to light in the course of a study of the poet's work. . . . [Child] had a peculiarly kind, soothing, encouraging voice, when putting questions to a student whom he had learned to know would answer his questions on the text under discussion accurately. . . . But woe betide the unfortunate who had shown carelessness or inability in following the professor's lectures and comments! His voice then assumed a cutting sarcastic tone. With little sniffs and "Umphs!," indescribable grunts, and unintelligible mutterings, he would lead the quaking student on by short, sharp questions into the most ridiculous and amazing assertions, and then suddenly overwhelm him by a tempestuous outburst, the memory of which often caused the delinquent to prepare himself for the recitations in that particular course with extreme care for a long while thereafter.[13]

The view from within the pale was a different one. A student who entered Child's classroom with some competence in the subject found a generous kindred spirit. Even the Professor's allegedly vague obliquities took on a point to the initiated, as is apparent in the following reminiscence by one of Child's most appreciative protégés, Francis Gummere:

"The reason why one comes to like Chaucer better than Spenser," said Mr. Child, in his cheery, conversational way,

to a certain class many years ago, "is that Chaucer always
has his feet on the ground, while Spenser—ah, well, you
know, Spenser is one of our greatest poets. . . ." "What did
he say?" gasped the man who made a point of accurate
notes.[14]

To audiences who did not have to face daily questions while the
course was in progress, or to pass an examination at the end of it,
Child's love and understanding of his favorite works could add a great
deal of delight to an experience which for many people was still a fresh
discovery. Gummere describes such an occasion in another of his nos-
talgic articles on Child. Enrolled in what Gummere describes as an
"omnibus course,"

We [the class] were tantalized with the too brief glimpses of
Chaucer and Shakespeare as Child interpreted them to us,
and as no other man then living could have done; and we
showed plainly our desire for more. The course had to make
its predestined way; but he told us that if we cared to sacrifice
an extra hour each week, say the gorged and lazy hour after
what was then midday dinner in "Memorial," he should read
us the *Canterbury Tales* and a fair bit of Shakespeare. "You
may bring a friend, if you like," he added, and appointed his
first reading in the familiar little room. But when he came
to keep the tryst, he found stairway and hall fairly filled with
a gentle mob which awaited the chance of a seat for perhaps
every fourth man. His score of students had become a crowd
of listeners; like another Moses, he had to lead his flock about
the building until he got habitation in a room which is now
sacred to the faculty. All the seats there were occupied and
remained so to the end of the course. Some of those hearers
can never forget Mr. Child's combined pleasure and amaze-
ment as he made his way through the first crowd; can never
forget those readings—the quiet but effective tones, the sympathy which made Chaucer so fresh, so rich, such "God's
plenty" indeed; and, above all, the pause and the slow wiping
of spectacles after the "And so I am, I am," of Cordelia to
Lear.[15]

New Configurations:
Graduate Programs, Women

Graduate students formed another congenial group of Child supporters and of appreciators of the great works of English literature. Harvard's graduate instruction in English studies became more systematic with the reform of the graduate program in the 1870s. The Master of Arts then became an earned degree rather than a sort of formality, as it had been earlier, when a candidate need only wait three years after taking his Bachelor's, send in five dollars, and receive a Master's. Child held one of these himself. The earlier procedure seemed designed to demonstrate that the candidate was still serious about his studies after three years, or cared about them five dollars' worth at any rate. The new model, however, required considerable additional work and a special examination.

Aside from the revised requirements for the M.A., the big news on the Harvard graduate scene in the 1880s was the installation of the Ph.D. degree. The *Catalogue* stressed the standards to be upheld:

> The degree of Ph.D. . . . is given, not for the mere reason of faithful study for a prescribed time, or in fulfillment of a determinate programme, and never for miscellaneous studies, but on the ground of long study and high attainment in a special branch of learning, manifested not only by examination, but by a thesis which must be presented and accepted before the candidate is admitted to examination, and must show an original treatment of a fitting subject, or give evidence of independent research.[16]

The Ph.D. was of course a German degree, and its adoption in America reflects the pervasive Germanic influence on American education. Charles W. Eliot, president of Harvard since 1869, had spent some time at the German universities before he took office and had been impressed by many aspects of the system. In Germany the Ph.D. degree represented a strenuous effort, requiring, as did its English-speaking descendants, a substantial thesis.

The first American Ph.D. degrees—three of them at once—were granted at Yale in 1861. By 1876, the year Johns Hopkins University was founded on a very Germanic model and with a strong emphasis on graduate studies, the Ph.D. was already offered by twenty-five American institutions. Graduate enrollment went up, naturally, as American scholars who might have gone to Germany for their degrees stayed at home instead, and as others entered graduate school who would not have done so had they had to leave the country. From an estimated figure of just under two hundred in 1870, American graduate students in the liberal arts increased to almost three thousand in 1890.

Harvard's first Ph.D. in English literature was awarded in 1876 and thus predated the formal establishment of the program. The candidate, Robert Grant, can be seen as a transitional figure, something of a well-rounded man of letters, rather than as the professional academician with which the Ph.D. rapidly became associated as more and more colleges began to require it as a qualification for higher-ranking teaching poisitions. Grant had taken his B.A. at Harvard in 1873 but felt dissatisfied with his performance; having put more emphasis on his social than his intellectual life, he felt a need for redress, and, as he explains twenty years later, he then spent three years as "a candidate for the degree of Ph.D., being one of the earliest applicants . . . living in Boston and coming out now and then to consult Professor Child, whose valuable, friendly counsel I have always remembered with gratitude."[17] Grant's studies included German and Italian literature as well, and he recalls being examined in Dante by James Russell Lowell, with Child sitting in. His thesis, under Child's direction, summarized theories about Shakespeare's sonnets. On completing this degree, he went on for another, entering Harvard's law school and earning a Bachelor of Laws in 1879. He then became an author, writing some thirty-odd volumes of essays, fiction, and poetry during a long career.

The question of admitting women loomed at Harvard as it did elsewhere and was approached, as in England, by a Women's Educational Association; the name was slightly different, but the intent was the same. In the mid-1870s, thanks to the efforts of this body, women might sit for either a preliminary or an advanced examination at Harvard, with successful candidates in either category receiving a certificate. The preliminary examination included English, French, physical geography, arithmetic, algebra through quadratic equations, plane geometry, and history, all subjects which must be presented; a choice of either elementary botany or elementary physics; and, as an additional language, a choice of German, Latin, or Greek.[18] The examination was given during seven days, spread over two weeks. Not surprisingly, candidates were few, two to four certificates constituting a good year. Survivors might go on to prepare for the advanced examination, a more specialized affair. In the language division, for example, one could offer two languages chosen from English, French, German, Italian, Latin, or Greek.

With this system, which was a temporary one as women were shortly to be found taking separate courses and adding up their credits like other American students, we happen to have an approximation of the British pattern of demonstrating one's fitness for a degree at one blow. The degree in question here was, of course, merely a certificate, but it was a highly respected one.

Respect or no respect, however, women naturally pressed for the degree and for what one might call full citizenship. At Harvard the means to this end were achieved through the establishment of Radcliffe College. The provision of a residential, collegiate context for women who would otherwise spend their years of preparation in an academic hand-to-mouth fashion was a large step forward.

Editorial and Scholarly Undertakings

To Child's teaching duties were added, fairly frequently, those of an administrator, for he spent many years as chairman of the rapidly growing English Department and also served in the 1890s as chairman of the Division of Modern Languages, to which the English Department belonged. The quantity and the quality of the scholarly work he produced thus become even more surprising. Asked how he managed to do it, Child once replied that he kept the work ready on his desk and when he found any scrap of time, even as little as twenty minutes, he sat down to it.

The direction of Child's endeavors was set by his interests within the field of English philology, which interests tended to go back in time, toward the earlier phases both of the linguistic forms and of the patterns of literature, e.g., dramatic, narrative, which had developed in the more recent centuries. He was also drawn to an appreciation of the individual talent, or individual genius perhaps, as seen in his love for Shakespeare and Chaucer. His equally strong passion for the anonymous folk ballad might seem to fit in rather strangely here, but in fact Child often treated the ballad as though it were the product of some single creative urge, almost as though the anonymous ballad-maker had a definable personality. This sensitivity enabled him to navigate with a clear inner certainty of what was and what was not by his own standards a folk ballad, a matter to be dealt with a bit later.

These preferences were modified by the circumstances in which Child worked. First, the need of the times was for editions, for simply getting the body of English literature into print in accurate form. This is the need which publishers sensed and with which scholars, including Child, would concur. Second, the texts needed for the kind of study Child preferred were not easily accessible to an American. The texts were across the ocean. This last problem was one which Child approached in two ways—either to work from a dependable printed edition to which he did have access, or to enlist the aid of colleagues more fortunately located.

In using the first of these methods, Child generally chose as good a text as he could find and then added to its usefulness by placing the work in its historical context and supplying as much assistance with the language problems as space would permit. Child's first scholarly publication, *Four Old Plays*, described above, reflects his principles here. In the 1850s Child continued this type of contribution by supervising the preparation of several titles in the "British Poets" series carried on by Houghton Mifflin. His own major contribution here was a five-volume edition (later reprinted in other formats) of the poetry of Spenser.

This work, which remained the standard American edition from its appearance in 1855 through the rest of the century, was based on the 1839 edition of George Hilliard, but Child greatly expanded the philological apparatus and added a sketch of Spenser's life, using the latest archival discoveries up to that point. (For the second edition, in 1859, he conscientiously draws his readers' attention to some newly published speculations on the identity of Spenser's mysterious Rosalind.) Child was able to consult earlier editions of Spenser to settle any textual questions that rose in his mind, and in general he had reason to feel pleased with his work. Spenser is, after all, of the major writers through Shakespeare much the easiest to edit, as far as the authority of the text is concerned. Spenser wished his writing to live; he respected

University College, London, was founded in the early nineteenth century to bring higher education to any student who could meet the entrance requirements and pay the fees, with none of the religious barriers which then obtained at Oxford and Cambridge. Devoted to innovation and common sense, University College furthered knowledge in strange new directions, such as English language and literature. (Drawing of the original building in Bloomsbury, still the heart of the College, by H. O. Corfiato, reproduced in H. Hale Bellot, *University College, London, 1826–1926* [London: University of London Press, 1929].)

The first professors of English had to come from somewhere, even though no formal training was available in the subject. Henry Morley, here aged 25, started out as a medical doctor, with English literature as an avocation. (Portrait from Henry Shaen Solly, *The Life of Henry Morley, LL.D.* [London: Edward Arnold, 1898].)

Henry Morley in professorial dignity, from his obituary notice in the *Illustrated London News* of May 19, 1894. During his 24 years at University College, Morley, a pillar of the faculty, brought recognition both to his department and to the new discipline he professed. His busy lecture schedule at University College and elsewhere prevented his completing the history of English literature, *English Writers*, which he worked on all his life. (Illustration courtesy of the Mary Evans Picture Library.)

Germany in the nineteenth century had become a mecca for scholars interested in philology. Francis James Child, on leave from his teaching duties at Harvard, here appears in German student costume; the drawing was a gift from Child to Joseph T. Atkinson of Baltimore, whom Child met at the University of Göttingen in 1850–51. (Courtesy of the Harvard University Archives.)

Professor Child as his students remembered him—assertive, energetic, quick to reward the diligent and embarrass the dilatory. Child taught rhetoric at Harvard for many years, working English literature into his syllabi whenever he could; during the later part of his career he was best known for his course in Shakespeare. His life work, collecting and editing English and Scottish folk ballads, was carried on in spare moments outside the classroom. (Courtesy of the Harvard University Archives.)

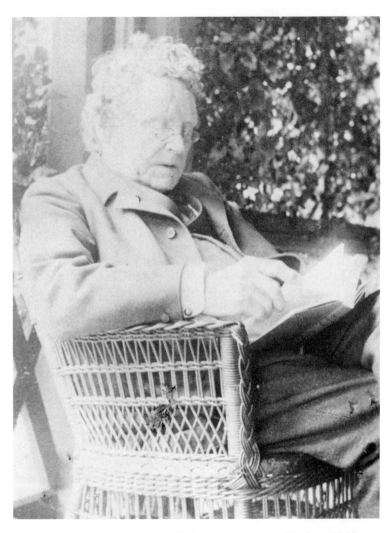

A summer day on the front porch of 67 Kirkland Street; some of Professor Child's roses are looking over his shoulder. Here Child welcomed his colleagues, among them James Russell Lowell, and his favorite students, among them Francis B. Gummere and George Lyman Kittredge. (Courtesy of the Harvard University Archives.)

A Harvard examination in English, 1892–93, reflecting what Child's department saw as the basics of literature and rhetoric. (More advanced courses covered literary history, Anglo-Saxon, and major writers.) Much of the literature included here was quite modern, as close in time to readers of that day as, say, the early poetry of T. S. Eliot is to our own. In the rhetoric section, students grappled with the distinction between "shall" and "will" and other familiar demons. Marginal comments, presumably written by the anonymous examinee, suggest that June 6, 1893 was a fine day outdoors. (Courtesy of the Harvard University Archives.)

To L—— with this

1892-93.

ENGLISH A.

I.

[Ninety minutes.]

Under each head write to the point, and as briefly as is compatible with clearness and fulness.

Women or men character

1. Miss Austen's range and her limitations.

2. Miss Austen's relations (a) with Mrs. Radcliffe; (b) with Richardson; (c) with Miss Burney.

3. Miss Edgeworth's place in literary history.

4. Miss Ferrier's novels.

5. In what sense Scott was, and in what sense he was not, an extemporaneous writer.

6. Scott's leading trait as man and as writer.

7. One of Scott's best drawn characters.

8. A scene from "The Vicar of Wakefield."

9. A brief account of "The Deserted Village."

II.

[One hour.]

1. What is meant by "consistency in the point of view" in description? What two important variations of the general rule are there?

2. What is the subject-matter of exposition? How does "division" complete the work begun by "definition"? Give an example of "definition"; one of "division."

3. What was Burke's *general* proposition in his speech on the "Thirteen Resolutions"? On what more specific issue did he really rest his case? Analyze the question as it presented itself to Burke, developing it from the most general to the most specific issue.

4. What is a "brief"? Explain its elements specifically.

5. State the kinds of evidence in the order of their importance.

III.

[Thirty minutes.]

1. (a) Discuss the rhetorical value of Climax as an aid to Clearness and Force.

(b) Discuss other methods of arrangement by which Clearness and Force may be gained.

2. Explain the use of *shall* and *will* to express futurity.

3. Rewrite the following sentences, giving your reasons for all the changes which you make : —

(a) Here and there I saw blue smoke curling upward, and occasionally the sound of an axe on a neighboring hillside was heard, and these were the only signs of life.

(b) It is pleasant to listen at a church-door, like Faust, and hear the roll of an organ from the door-steps on these fine days in May.

Final. 1893. *June 6*

An entrance to Harvard Yard (Johnson Gate, erected 1890) near the turn of the century. During Child's 50-year association with his alma mater, the academic scene grew more flexible, here coming to include bicycles, women, and—not visible to the artist—the elective system, which through the previous decades had loosened up the traditional curriculum and allowed the growth of new departments of knowledge, English studies among them. (Illustration by W. H. Hyde for Edward S. Martin, "Undergraduate Life at Harvard," *Scribner's Magazine*, May 1897.)

From a] AGE 19. [*Daguerreotype.*

PROFESSOR DAVID MASSON.
BORN 1822.

AVID MASSON, Professor of Rhetoric and English Literature in the University of Edinburgh, who began his literary career at the age of nineteen, as editor of a Scotch provincial newspaper, was appointed

AGE 29.
From a Photo. by Dr. Diamond, Edinburgh.

to the Chair of English Language and Literature at the University College, London, in 1852. He retired from his post in October, 1865, having been appointed Professor of

Rhetoric and English Literature in the University of Edinburgh. He contributed numerous articles to the *Quarterly, National, British Quarterly,* and *North British Reviews,* and to the " Encyclopædia Britannica," and his papers on Carlyle's " Latter-day Pamphlets," " Dickens and Thackeray," " Rabelais," etc., are the best known. His other works are so numerous that several pages of this Magazine

From a Photo. by] AGE 43. [*John Watkins.*

would be required to give them in anything like detail, and we regret that space will not permit us to do so. A committee, headed by Lord Robertson, is preparing a suitable testimonial to Dr. Masson, in recognition of his important services to English literature.

PRESENT DAY.
From a Photo. by J. Horsburgh, Edinburgh.

David Masson is given a full-scale media-star treatment by the *Pall Mall Magazine* in 1901. Professor Masson came to embody the Victorian ideal of the public figure; radiating authority and good cheer, he convinced his students that they had embarked upon a valuable course of study. The text here lists some of Masson's contributions to periodicals and to the *Encyclopedia Britannica* but fails to mention the biography of Milton for which he is remembered today. (Courtesy of the Mary Evans Picture Library.)

Professor Masson in his study, generating swirls of pipesmoke and manuscript pages. Less bound by tradition than the established English universities, the University of Edinburgh had already let snippets of English literature into her curriculum under the heads of rhetoric and belles lettres. Masson enlarged the territory considerably. This sketch by William Hole was drawn for the University of Edinburgh's tercentenary celebration in 1884. (Courtesy of Edinburgh University Library.)

History of English Literature

world. Milton's idea of the world, Heaven and Hell, may be best described by a diagram. He wrote "Paradise Lost" with the Ptolemaic view of the Universes.

HEAVEN OR

THE

E M P Y R E A N

CHAOS   CHAOS

H E L L

The outside circle represents the original infinity of Space; the line through the centre divides this into Heaven and Chaos. Heaven was the special seat of God, though he ranged through the whole infinitude of Space. As God's ministers in Heaven there were angels. These were divided into Archades and there seem to have been archangels among them. Of these 7 are named, four of

While thousands of teachers of Milton have drawn this diagram of the setting of *Paradise Lost*, following the explanations in the poem itself, Masson was one of the first. This version appears in the class notes taken by J. Allen Gray, a student in Masson's course in 1868–69. The concentric circles are the planets in their spheres, with Earth in the center; Hell is the darkest ellipse at the bottom, to which Lucifer and his angels fell. Later, Masson's diagram became more elaborate. A notebook from 1887–1888 includes the bridge from Hell to Earth and even accounts for the area outside the circle, "Ab-original Infinitude." (Courtesy of the Edinburgh University Library.)

Sir George Reid, who painted this portrait of Masson upon the occasion of the latter's retirement, had once shocked the public by his unorthodox treatment of light and shade, but sensibilities shifted with the times and Reid was at this point—1896—president of the Royal Scottish Academy. Masson was associated with the visual arts much of his life, having married into an artistic family and formed friendships in the 1840s with the Pre-Raphaelite painters. (Courtesy of the Scottish National Portrait Gallery.)

During his 30 years as Professor of Rhetoric and English Literature, Masson taught nearly 5000 students in his best-known course, a year-long excursion into rhetoric, literary history, and selected readings. The students in this drawing of the University of Edinburgh's Old Quad, made a few years after Masson's retirement, would have taken a similar course under Masson's successor, George Saintsbury. (Drawing from *The Student*, 1898–99, reproduced in D. B. Horn, *A Short History of the University of Edinburgh 1556–1880*, 1967. Courtesy of the Edinburgh University Press.)

A retiring personality though not a recluse, Walter William Skeat usually avoided the spotlight but found himself incorporated into an ornamental border, here enlarged, in the *Illustrated London News* of March 19, 1910. The accompanying article described Skeat's accomplishments to a larger reading public than that to which he was accustomed; by this late point in his career these included his dictionaries, his work for the Early English Text Society, and his editions of Chaucer and of *Piers Plowman*. (Courtesy of the Mary Evans Picture Library.)

A contemporary tourist's guidebook shows Christ's College, Cambridge, as something of a medieval fortress. Here, following the established curriculum, Skeat as an undergraduate excelled in theology and mathematics. When he returned some years later as a lecturer in mathematics, Skeat slipped English literature through the ramparts by establishing, out of his own pocket, an annual prize for the best essay on an assigned topic in that field. (Drawing from *Jarrold's Illustrated Guide to Cambridge*, 1911).

Professor Skeat relaxing with two fellow lexicographers: Joseph Wright of the *English Dialect Dictionary*, at left, shortest beard; James Murray of the *Oxford English Dictionary*, center, longest beard; and Skeat, intermediately bearded, at right. The picture was taken in Murray's garden in Oxford, probably about 1910. (Reproduced by kind permission of K. M. Elisabeth Murray.)

Skeat in his study. Many types of metal-tipped pens were in use by the end of the century; quill pens made of goose feathers, however, were still cheap and plentiful, and Skeat evidently preferred them, judging from the three on the table as well as the one in his hand. Typewriters were found only in the most up-to-date business offices, and printers ordinarily set type from handwritten copy. (Photograph from *The Academy*, July 15, 1899.)

During the last two decades of the nineteenth century, the growing number of women admitted to higher education was accompanied by a growing enrollment in English courses. Perhaps not surprisingly, all four professors dealt with in this book were strong advocates of women's education. This young lady, diligently reading two books at once, was drawn by Orson Lowell to accompany an article by Margaret Sherwood, "Undergraduate Life at Vassar," in *Scribner's Magazine*, June 1898.

the permanence of print, and he appears to have seen most of his works quite painstakingly through the press, bizarre spellings and all.

For the same series, Child was asked to prepare an edition of Chaucer's poetry, but here Child objected. The situation was quite different. Chaucer had not seen an authentic version of his works through the press, since printing had not been invented in the western world during Chaucer's lifetime; the manuscripts were transmitted by hand, one copyist following another. The surviving manuscripts of Chaucer's works were in the mid nineteenth century in a state not exactly chaotic—people knew where they were—but were certainly inconvenient for scholars. Each manuscript, and fragment of manuscript, is after all unique; different scribes make different errors, as Chaucer was himself gloomily aware in his poem to his less-than-perfectly-competent scribe Adam. To discern the author's intentions through this kind of veil, an editor needs to consult as many as possible of the surviving manuscripts before he can give the public what he feels to be a reasonably accurate version of a work. For Child, the texts simply were not available for comparison. The surviving manuscripts were scattered into many and distant collections, some of which were not hospitable to inquiring scholars. (The joys of photocopying were far in the future.) Nor had any substantial number of transcriptions been published of the individual manuscripts—at least, not in the 1850s. (Throughout the final decades of the century this situation was continually improved. Furnivall in fact founded the Chaucer Society, which had as its purpose the publication of Chaucerian manuscripts, in 1868 as a result of Child's urging British scholars to bring to light their national treasures. Furnivall's six-text edition of the *Canterbury Tales* was published in 1875.)

Child, having declined an editing job he could not have done well, retained his interest in Chaucer and his wish to further studies in this field; so he turned instead to certain problems of Chaucer's language. "Observations on the Language of Chaucer," as the results were modestly titled, first appeared in the *Memoirs* of the American Academy of Arts and Sciences in 1862; later a condensed and rearranged version was incorporated by the phoneticist and linguist Alexander John Ellis in his *On Early English Pronunciation* (Chaucer Society, Philological Society, and Early English Text Society, 1869–89).

This brief treatise made a resounding impact upon the scholarly world. Setting out to settle questions concerning the number of syllables in Middle English words, a matter intrinsic to the study of Chaucer's versification, Child presents clearly tabulated evidence, much of it in the form of lists of words: Anglo-Saxon nouns, French adjectives, etc. Careful attention is paid to contractions and to the elision of final vowels. (Child did not rediscover Chaucer's final *e*; this vowel, or rather the fact that it had been pronounced and therefore constituted an additional syllable, had been reclaimed by a succession of editors in the eighteenth century. Child was adding a refinement, the fact that under certain circumstances the *e* was not pronounced.) For the purpose of these tabulations, Child used the Thomas Wright edition of the *Canterbury Tales* (1847–51), based on Harleian Manuscript 7334. To rely on a single manuscript of a single poem was not, he felt, an ideal state of things, but it was as good as he could get; and, as he pointed out, this work in this form includes 17,000 lines of verse, allowing a reasonably good sample.

A continuation of this study, "Observations on the Language of Gower," appeared shortly afterward in order to provide some perspective on the Chaucerian patterns. Although the purpose of the work is linguistic, Child cannot help bringing a critical focus temporarily to bear and noting that, by comparison to the richness of Chaucer, Gower's writing shows "a poverty of expression and a want of ease."

Child and the Ballads

In the course of his career, Child made two ballad collections, a little one and a big one, although the little one is quite substantial and diminishes only by comparison. Compiled as part of the "English Poets" series mentioned earlier and issued in eight volumes in 1857, this earlier effort relied on the printed sources available at the time and bears the title of *English and Scottish Ballads*. Child's subsequent magnum opus, reaching farther back into time to utilize manuscript sources rather than printed ones, appeared in volume after volume from the early 1880s until 1898, two years after Child's death; the final collection was prepared for the press by Kittredge. The title of this work, *The English and Scottish Popular Ballads*, enables it to be distinguished from its predecessor by the definite article *The*, which word, according

to Sigurd Bernhard Hustvedt, was "put there deliberately"[19] and is in-
dicative of Child's goal of rounding up the entire canon. The word
"popular," also added to the later collection, refers to the ballads' derivation from the people and does not utilize the present-day connotation of "well-liked"; these are not, in other words, a collection of
particular favorites for the assembling of which some other less-than-
favorites had to be left out.

The English and Scottish Popular Ballads attempted not only to
follow authentic manuscript sources but to include every available version of every ballad. The collection thus contains 305 different titles,
arranged in categories of Child's devising, and each title appears with
its own family of variant versions, all reproduced in full. Mixed in with
this complex but clearly arranged text are Child's notes and comments.
He draws our attention to unusual features, makes analogies with other
ballads in this collection and other ballads in other languages, points
out themes, speculates on dates and origins, and generally acts as a
cheery and knowledgeable guide.

The volumes thus achieve an unusual degree of attraction for the
casual browser—not, admittedly, the first aim of a scholarly work, but
perhaps in this case having something to do with this collection's wide
influence in fields other than literary history and philology. The ballads
can become a part of the casual reader's life very easily. One can spend
an odd ten minutes reading several versions of, say, "Mary Hamilton,"
number 173, enjoying the experience in three phases—the stark story
itself; the different emphases created by the variants (fifteen of them,
not counting a few separate odd stanzas); and finally Child's factual but
conversational observations—without seriously derailing one's plans for
the day. For the casual reader, in fact, Child' collection is often more
enjoyable in small helpings than in large ones. This self-contained
quality of the individual items also appeals to the editors of anthologies.
Systematic collections based on literary history must of course include
ballads as a significant part of this history; other collections of poetry
or literature in general, include ballads for their own sake. Thus generations of readers, schoolchildren for example, have come upon "Lord
Randall" or "Sir Patrick Spens," presented usually in only one version,
with notes often deriving from Child's. The ballads have come back
into the English-speaking heritage.

Child never got around to explaining exactly what he was collecting. A preface to this effect was to have been added to the final

volume, but Child died before he could write it. The criteria for inclusion or exclusion may be worked out nevertheless, based on the ballads which were in fact included or excluded.

An early date was an essential qualification, for Child saw the traditional folk ballad as one transmitted orally, polluted as little as possible from printed sources. Thus Shakespeare's Autolycus, welcomed so cheerily with his pack of broadside ballads by the villagers of Bohemia eager to buy and sing this musical ware, would represent for Child a corrupter of the pure folk impulse. Commercial ballad-writers from the Elizabethan times onward were to Child mere hacks—inartistic, exploitative of any traditional materials they might happen across and liable to combine verses from different sources with no regard for the integrity of the originals. Their products were doubly dangerous in that they might be memorized by their purchasers, sung to audiences, and thus get back into the oral tradition in a degenerate form.

The texts Child preferred, then, were old manuscript collections which had been written down by private antiquarian hobbyists, straight from the singers' mouths, at some point in time before the tide of cheap printing had begun to alter the songs' traditional forms and interfere with the natural evolution represented by their variant versions. Pre-sixteenth century would certainly seem safe, as the printing press reached England only in 1475. Print and its culture moved slowly, however, and in some remote parts of England and Scotland the original ballads remained inviolate for many generations longer. The Percy Manuscript, for example, of which we shall hear more, had been written down from oral sources in the mid-seventeenth century. A few ballads admitted to the canon do have an exceptionally late date—"Mary Hamilton," for example, mentioned above, dates only from the eighteenth century. "It is remarkable that one of the very latest of the Scottish popular ballads should be one of the very best," observes Child, quite ungrudgingly; he did not try to bend the facts to fit his theories and was willing to admit an exception.

Besides having (almost always) an early date, the "Child ballad" is identifiable as a specific literary category. It might be simpler to list the things a Child ballad isn't. It is not a short lyric poem, say, a woeful one made to one's mistress's eyebrow; not in fact any poem with a definite author, so that Wordsworth and Coleridge's *Lyrical Ballads* could not have been admitted, nor could the newly written sentimental "ballads" so often sung in Victorian parlors, even though these latter often incorporated willow trees and other traditional motifs. (Child in fact wrote one of these himself, "The Lass of the Pamunky," which he included in his personal Civil War effort, a small songbook titled *War Songs for Freemen*, published in Boston in 1862 and sent marching south with several regiments from the area. The Pamunky, or Pamunkey, is a river in Virginia; the story concerns a soldier being nursed back to health.)

The traditional ballad of the Child type, then, was a narrative, telling its story simply, often with abrupt transitions and dialogue; it might be based on a historical event, and it might relate to other ballads as part of a cycle, but neither of these attributes is required. The supernatural was often an important element. It could not, however, be introduced gratuitously. Ghosts, as Child explains, should

> have a fair reason for walking . . . In popular fictions [i.e., the traditional ballad] the motive for their leaving the grave is to ask back plighted troth, to be relieved from the inconveniences caused by the excessive grief of the living, to put a stop to the abuse of children by stepmothers, to repair an injustice done in the flesh, to fulfill a promise; at the least, to announce the visitant's death.[20]

The process of assembling all this material is exhausting even to contemplate. Child was based thousands of miles from the texts he wanted to examine. Frequent trips to the British Isles were financially infeasible; Harvard did what it could to assist its faculty's research, but the budget was a slim one. Child made the most of this type of opportunity when he got it, in 1873 managing not only to examine manuscript collections in the British Museum but to make personal contact with Furnivall in London and William Macmath in Edinburgh, each of whom was to become a close collaborator as the work progressed. For the most part, however, Child depended on an increasingly complex network of helpers, working by remote control, so to speak.

A useful aid in this enterprise, as Child got it under way in the 1870s, was the existence of his 1857 *English and Scottish Ballads*. People could see at once what sort of thing was wanted. In fact, many of the actual ballads in the two collections are the same, although the earlier work made no attempt to include every version and was based upon less authentic printed sources. Of the 305 titles included in *The English and Scottish Popular Ballads*, only 90 had not also appeared in *English and Scottish Ballads*. A substantial number of titles from *English and Scottish Ballads*, 115, had in the meantime been dropped; Child felt on further investigation that these were later inventions, not true popular ballads from the oral tradition, or that they belonged in some literary category other than that of the narrative.

Child's helpers, ranging from eminent foreign scholars to simpler folk willing to check a reference or locate a manuscript fragment far from the compiler's study on Kirkland Street, numbered in the scores and sent to Child, as the years went on, enough correspondence to fill thirty-one volumes in the Harvard archives.[21] As the successive parts of the collection appeared, Child's lists of those to whom he owed thanks grew longer and longer. Some of these acknowledgees appear elsewhere in the present study, indicating once again the small and interdependent world of nineteenth-century scholarship. In an 1882 volume Child mentioned, among many others, Walter William Skeat and Henry Bradshaw of Cambridge (both of whom reappear in chapter five, the latter assisting the former); John Payne Collier, who has figured more dubiously in chapter one; and Edward Arber, the former student of Henry Morley, in 1882 at the University of Birmingham. A further category of helpers was made up of Child's American friends, in particular friends able to travel abroad with some frequency; Child gives special thanks to "Mr. James Russell Lowell, Minister of the United States at London."

Of Child's long-distance colleagues the top two, Furnivall and Macmath, gave of their time and energy in ways typical of their quite different personalities. Furnivall's general exuberance and his many literary connections made him a natural contact point. Near the beginning of his quest, for example, Child put an announcement in the British journal *Notes and Queries* asking that scholars willing to share ballad lore get in touch with him through Furnivall. Furnivall also assisted Child in sending out a circular to the clergymen and schoolmasters of Scotland—two occupations which Furnivall and Child apparently thought sufficiently literate and also sufficiently close to the lives of the people—in search of any ballads or fragments of ballads which might have remained alive in the folk tradition. This last attempt was disappointing; virtually nothing turned up; but this lack of success confirmed Child's impression that the kind of material he wanted could best be found in the older manuscripts.

It was with regard to manuscripts that Furnivall performed his most dramatic service to Child's efforts. As something of an astonishing victory, since the attempt had been made before, Furnivall in the 1860s acquired permission to publish the Percy Manuscript, a mid-seventeenth-century collection of early ballads. This treasure had already led a life crowded with incident. It had been found by Thomas Percy, later Bishop of Dromore, in the parlor of his friend Humphrey Pitt in Shropshire; here the manuscript, far from occupying a place of honor, was being used by the maids to light the fire. Pages from both the front and the back had already been torn away. Percy asked for and was given the remainder, took it away, and sent it to a bookbinder who in trimming the edges cut off some of the top and bottom lines of writing. As if these deprivations were not enough, the manuscript then underwent alteration at the hands of Percy himself, who, having become genuinely fond of the songs, undertook to improve them, and in bringing out an edition in 1765 (*Reliques of Ancient English Poetry*) he added, deleted, and polished with considerable disregard for the integrity of the pieces. By the nineteenth century, scholars had become both curious and suspicious about the original. The heirs of Bishop Percy denied access to it, and Furnivall's circumventing this obstacle was a complex procedure involving repeated attempts, fortunate timing, the assistance of mutual friends, and a bit of bribery. The story is told, from Furnivall's standpoint entirely, in the introduction to the edition of the manuscript which Furnivall and John Wesley Hales (a Shakespeare and Milton scholar and an early proponent of the teaching of English) published in 1867–68. This work, in four volumes, was dedicated to Child—a compliment which Child returned by dedicating *The English and Scottish Popular Ballads* to Furnivall because, as Child then said, his collection could not have been made had he not had the Percy ballads in their original form at his disposal.

Child's other major colleague, Macmath, differed from Furnivall in that he had virtually no other literary projects in hand except the collecting of ballads. Macmath held a full-time job as a law scrivener which did not allow him a great deal of leisure time, while Furnivall, though originally trained in the law and for a few years a practicing barrister, had devoted his life to scholarly labors and subsisted on a minimal salary as a teacher of evening classes at the Working Men's College, London. Macmath, however, in his bits of spare time managed to accomplish some remarkable things. He found and transcribed manuscripts in private collections, in archives, in it would seem any depository in which a scrap of old paper could hide itself. (Macmath's earliest communication with Child concerned a ballad fragment discovered in a collection of law papers dating from 1590.) One pictures Macmath methodically ransacking the garrets of Edinburgh. At one point, when the library assembled by Walter Scott at Abbotsford proved to contain a rich vein of manuscript ballads, Macmath devoted his summer holidays—three weeks a year, for three years running—to searching and copying this material. His training as a scrivener meant that his accuracy could be depended upon, and he wrote, of course, a clear and beautiful hand.

Macmath's relationship to Child is a curious one, as Reppert has pointed out in his Harvard dissertation of 1953. Macmath was neither a coeditor nor an employee—simply a volunteer helper, like many others in the project, but on a very large scale. Child did reimburse Macmath for costs incurred in finding or transcribing the texts he supplied, a procedure which brought about their only quarrel when one job ran much higher than estimated,[22] but Macmath's basic motive seems to have been simply a longing to see the old ballads accurately in print. His love of the genre sprang from direct exposure to them, for ballads were known and sung by the older members of his own family. Macmath's aunt, in fact, Miss Jane Webster, supplied Child's collection with sixteen variant versions and thus makes a rare direct connection between *The English and Scottish Popular Ballads* and the elusive folk memory.

Child's Career: New and Old

During Child's lifetime, English studies became a solid part of the American educational system, installed securely at the elementary and secondary levels and expanding briskly at the college level. The new subject was by the 1890s no longer new; its value was no longer open to question, and debate centered on exactly what should be taught and how this teaching should be done. Child had not taken a large part in the organizing, speechmaking, and general persuasion which accompanied this expansion, though he regarded its results with good cheer. He had put the first English courses into the Harvard curriculum on his own, and he devoted his energies to his own teaching and his strenuous research.

Child's most visible descendants, his pedagogical children and grandchildren, would include the many fledgling folklorists and ballad-collectors who were attracted to Harvard by Child's international fame and also by the books and manuscripts which Harvard acquired in order to help Child's research—many items of which were of course spotted and ordered by Child himself. The collection was and remains a significant one. Harvard folklorists of these later generations include Kittredge, who followed his mentor into many rapidly diversifying fields, and a bit later Fred Norris Robinson, Stith Thompson, and John Avery Lomax—the latter a pioneer in American song tradition, the collector of "Git Along, Little Dogies," and the father of Alan Lomax, also a folklore specialist trained at Harvard.

But to see Child as a founding father of folklore would be somewhat misleading. Specialization has naturally brought about changes in emphasis. Today's ballad-collector, for example, may well sally forth with a tape recorder to catch the creative folk impulse actually at work among immigrant fruit pickers, Appalachian miners, or—who knows—workers in silicone chip factories. Child himself focused on the past, on the old manuscripts, not because he denigrated the present, but because the past in his day was an unknown country; and large areas needed to be mapped. The past is where the excitement was. Child's quest may seem a particularly nebulous one, seeking as he did a literature transmitted orally by long-dead singers, and yet he brought his findings into solid form, salvaging and giving a coherent niche to a portion of our literature which might otherwise have been collected haphazardly or not at all.

Child's teaching throughout his career remained centered on the priorities of English language and literature as he saw them. Students needed Anglo-Saxon, Chaucer, Shakespeare; first things first. In the last two years of his life he did teach a graduate seminar titled "The English and Scottish Popular Ballads" and thus bridged the gap into the present era, when a specialist of sufficient magnitude naturally assumes he will be given a course in that specialty. (And if this course is not forthcoming we tend to feel something is wrong with the system.) Child may well not have seen things that way. One can imagine him raising doubts; were students, even graduate students, really ready for a systematic approach to the ballads?

By this time, the mid-1890s, the indefatigable Child had slowed down somewhat. The Harvard catalogues of these years show, besides the ballad seminar, a continuing shift of what had been Child's courses into the custody of Kittredge. Child's remaining strength thus went to the final volume of *The English and Scottish Popular Ballads*. But this strength gave out; he became ill (a kidney problem) in the summer of 1896 and died on September 11, just as his students and colleagues were returning to Harvard for the fall semester. In what his contemporaries may have seen as a final example of Child's strong minded commonsense, his body was cremated, allowing one of the Boston newspapers to observe that "public knowledge of the cremation of the body of a man so distinguished as Professor Child is of incalculable value to the cause of cremation." This statement, along with many other obituary notices and memorials, was collected by Kittredge and put into a scrapbook now in the Harvard archives.[23] What was done with Child's ashes is not among the facts thus preserved. In view of the feeding preferences of roses, one cannot help harboring for a moment a doubtless spurious supposition. The roses at any rate survived their nurturer, as roses so often do in the ballads, to be done in by the Japanese beetle in the early decades of the twentieth century; and the house itself, where Child's students had found a warm welcome when they came to visit, continues its hospitality into the 1980s as the Kirkland Inn.[24]

4

David Masson (1822–1907), Edinburgh, and the *Life* of Milton

Like Morley, David Masson came to his Professorship of English from the variegated pursuit of journalism; like Child, he rose from a working-class background, his father having been a stonecutter in Aberdeen. Like both (and indeed like a large number of Victorians who achieved prominence in professions not even invented at the beginning of their century), he possessed energy and self-reliance to an extraordinary degree—was born, apparently, already grown-up and able to make his own decisions in a complex set of circumstances.

When he was thirteen years old Masson entered Marischal College, Aberdeen (which institution later, in 1860, became part of the University of Aberdeen upon merging with that city's King's College) and took his Master of Arts degree four years later, ranking first in his class.[1] Students in Scotland started young, although usually not quite that young, and the M.A. was the standard degree toward which the undergraduate worked during his four-year course. (English universities during the same period offered usually a three-year course leading to the Bachelor of Arts. This sort of diversity between the two systems lasted well into the twentieth century.)

Whatever the terminology, Masson had completed a challenging university degree by the time he was seventeen, and he did it on his own, tutoring private students in the evening to pay his college expenses. His world may have seemed at first a limited one. Aberdeen, on Scotland's east coast about a hundred miles north of Edinburgh, is in its special fashion a beautiful place, medieval at heart, its narrow streets running uphill from the harbor. A large proportion of its buildings are of granite—there was plenty of stone for Masson's father to cut, whenever the local economy encouraged building. But Masson

111

must have realized fairly early that wider ambitions required a wider context.

This ambition directed itself at first toward the Church of Scotland, a choice in harmony with many aspects of Masson's character. The national Church, which Scotland had retained as a separate entity despite the Act of Union with England in 1707 and which has no connection with the Church of England, being in fact Presbyterian, was a strong-minded body, valuing education and general alertness in her ministry. Masson's literary and historical interests, his energetic perception of all the aspects of any culture in which he found himself, and his enjoyment of a social circle of thoughtful and articulate colleagues would have been encouraged rather than smothered in a clerical life.

Masson accordingly went to Edinburgh in 1839 and spent three years in the study of divinity at the University. Here, too, he supported himself by tutoring. But through circumstances outside his control, the future he had envisioned began to cloud over. The strong-mindedness of the Church of Scotland could show itself as a capacity for fierce and unforgiving controversy, and in the early 1840s a major upheaval had the effect of diverting at least one of her aspiring ministers into other pursuits.

What occurred was the aptly named "Disruption."[2] The national Church divided itself into parties on the issue of ministers' being appointed to parishes without the approval of the congregations involved—an argument of ancient pedigree, in its main principles one of the differences between the Scottish Church and the Church of England—and also on the issue of the dividing of parishes in the fast-growing urban districts in order to minister more effectively to city populations. The last point mentioned, with some attendant ideas on the church's role in education, was a fairly new one and reflects some of the social changes typical of the nineteenth century. The arguments grew more and more complex and bitter, the schism deeper and more extensive. On surveying the scene, the modern reader may be tempted to take refuge in the simplifying observation that Presbyterians are very good at splitting asunder. Eventually some 450 of the national Church's 1,200 ministers left, taking with them what is variously estimated at one-fourth to one-third the membership, to form the Free Kirk of Scotland (a body which later underwent further modification). By this time Masson had taken a job in Aberdeen as editor of a weekly newspaper, *The Banner*, and in 1843 observed the climax of the controversy from a position outside the clerical life. As his daughter Flora Masson tells us, "On the great day of the Disruption he was again in Edinburgh, and present, as editor and reporter, in the gallery of St. Andrew's Church, from which he watched that memorable long line of the outgoing Ministers of the Church of Scotland."[3]

Masson Enters the World of Letters

Having made his decision for journalism, Masson at the age of barely twenty proved so competent an editor that in 1844 he was offered and accepted a job with the firm of R. and W. Chambers, publishers. Here, shuttling back to Edinburgh once again, Masson became part of an enterprise typical of the nineteenth-century publishing industry in that it both built upon and encouraged the growth of literacy in the population. Like a number of their colleagues, Willliam and Robert Chambers became an identifiable force in the shaping of the culture they lived in, publishing not only what they felt their customers would buy but what they felt they ought to buy. The two brothers had begun as booksellers in their teens, opening a stall of secondhand books and including in their stock their own schoolbooks; their family had sunk into difficulties and their plans for formal education had to be abandoned. They branched into bookbinding; they bought an old printing press; and they were on their way, specializing from their earliest years in Scottish history and topography and often writing their own material when needed.

The year 1844, when Masson joined the firm, was a fairly lively one, both for Chambers' publications in general and Masson's in particular. In the former category appears the first edition of *Chambers Cyclopedia of English Literature*, a work which was to be reissued, reedited, and augmented throughout the nineteenth century and on into the twentieth. Years later Masson was to list it among the books recommended for his own students at the University of Edinburgh. Robert Chambers, the more scholarly brother, edited it with Robert Carruthers of Inverness, a scholar whose interests also included Alexander Pope. A more dramatic publication of 1844, appearing anonymously and causing considerable controversy, was also the work of Robert Chambers—his *Vestiges of Creation*, in which the author examined the puzzling question of fossils and foreshadowed some of the evolutionary excitements of the later half of the century.

Masson's publications of 1844 were significant to him not because they precipitated a public stir—it is doubtful if they did—but because they constituted something of a foothold in the world of London letters. A childhood friend from Aberdeen, Alexander Bain, whose career was to continue to parallel Masson's to the extent of both eventually becoming English professors, was at the time in London, moving in circles which Masson upon arriving for a visit found very compatible. Bain introduced Masson to Thomas Carlyle, who by that time had already produced three of his best known works, *The French Revolution*, *Chartism*, and *On Heroes, Hero-Worship, and the Heroic in History*. As London's most prominent Scottish literary lion, Carlyle was encouraging to his countryman and in turn introduced Masson to the editor of *Fraser's Magazine*, in which many of Carlyle's essays made their first appearance. Masson was invited to submit some work, and did so; "On Emotional Culture" appeared in May of 1844 and a longer essay, "The Three Devils: Luther's, Milton's and Goethe's" the following December.

Meanwhile in Edinburgh, Masson, returning to his regular duties and taking charge of a "Miscellaneous and Historical" series for R. and W. Chambers, became an author whenever the need arose, turning out, for example, a brief but competent history of Rome. Masson's work was challenging and, perhaps as important, allowed him to live in Scotland. Masson's love for his native land can be seen in the many essays he later wrote about it and quite obviously in the fact that he spent the last half of his life there. But at this point in his career the lure of London persisted and brought him to a serious decision. He wanted to succeed in London; at the same time, he knew he could be leaving forever. As a sparsely populated country, her rocks and mountains heart-stoppingly beautiful but economically unproductive, Scotland has for centuries exported her people. There is simply no room in the system for all of them; people could in fact be considered one of the country's major resources, and money from overseas has mended ancestral Scottish roofs for many generations. But the economy closes in again behind those who leave. If they held a job, it is naturally given to someone else; and so, once settled abroad, except for visits the expatriates can seldom come home again. In 1847, when he packed his bags for the journey south, Masson may have felt he was crossing the Rubicon instead of the Tweed.

London Literary Circles

Masson thus arrived in London as a young man of twenty-five, versatile, reliable, and already of recognized literary abilities. The opportunities he found there grew, it seemed, every day. In the mid-nineteenth century the English-reading public was many times the figure for a hundred years earlier.[4] Not only was this public large and growing larger, but it fell into the kind of clearly defined categories that made the publishing of periodicals a challenging but often rewarding game of skill. An editor able to judge the taste of his readers and to supply a steady stream of material in accordance with it could increase his periodical's circulation, delight his publisher, and command a high salary. Mark Lemon, editor of *Punch*, was in the later stages of his career paid 1500 pounds a year; and his associate Douglas Jerold edited *Lloyd's Weekly Newspaper* in the 1850s for an annual salary of a thousand pounds. (Multiplying by forty or fifty, to get an approximation of today's buying power in American dollars, works fairly well here.) Dickens's success as a man of business is demonstrated by his skill in marketing his own product in *Household Words* and *All the Year Round*, and the salary he paid Henry Morley of five guineas a week (writers naturally earned less than editors) came from a prosperous enterprise. At the same time, of course, the world of letters did not guarantee riches, even to those who made a success of it. A Victorian seeking a fortune would have a better chance as a railway contractor. But editors and writers could enter the middle class and even become respectable; to depend for one's livelihood on writing for the general public, or for some segment of it, was not necessarily synonymous with a career of threadbare desperation.

Quite roughly, the publications which made up the freelance writer's market could be said to sort themselves out according to the frequency with which they were published. The quarterly reviews contained lengthy essays and appealed to an educated, even intellectual readership; the monthly magazines ran somewhat shorter articles and might include light reading in the form of poetry and fiction. (The fiction was often serialized.) The weeklies were by and large somewhat bouncier, and with their more frequent deadlines could of course be more up-to-date (one thinks of *Punch*), while the many daily newspapers allowed a choice from the sensational tabloids to the dignified *Times*.

Of this array, Masson's work found a welcome among the quarterlies and the monthly magazines, in particular those with liberal tendencies and/or a Scots accent. As well as the monthly *Fraser's Magazine*, founded in the 1830s, these included the *Quarterly Review*, founded by the Scottish publisher John Murray at the urging of Walter Scott in 1809; the *North British Review*, a voice of the Scottish Free Church; and the *Westminster Review*, founded in 1824 by the followers of Jeremy Bentham to advocate reform in church, state, and legislature. (In the same decade Bentham and his Utilitarian principles had been influential in the establishment of University College in London.) The 1840s was a time of considerable ferment, with social and political revolutions occurring in many countries of Europe, while the English wondered if their own comparatively minor upheavals—the Chartist demonstrations, for example—would boil over as well; and journalists found their readers eager to be informed and willing to ponder.

At Work in the British Museum

Masson provides a glimpse into the workaday mechanics of London's literary world in *The British Museum, Historical and Descriptive*, a handbook he wrote in the late 1840s for R. and W. Chambers. (For some years after he moved to London, Masson continued to supply his former employers with manuscripts on a variety of subjects.) Most of this volume is concerned with the museum's collections of Egyptian and other antiquities, but a few pages are given to the library facilities. Readers were then housed in rooms entered from the north side of the building, as the central domed Reading Room was not to be completed until the mid-1850s:

> Two of the largest apartments of the library of printed books have been specially fitted up as a reading room for the use of the public. . . . Here occasionally may be seen our authors and authoresses of greatest note glancing over rare books, making brief extracts, and hastening to be off; and here, more habitual and regular visitors, may be distinguished the young student reading professionally; the humble copyist driving his pen mechanically over the paper, and so earning his scanty and laborious livelihood; or, lastly, the conscientious writer of history, deep in the business of research.[5]

Ink and pens were provided by the Reading Room, Masson notes, but the reader could expect to be frustrated by "the very imperfect state of the catalogue." Another disadvantage of working in the Reading Room arose from one's companions. "One reader by you annoys you with his 'bassoon nose'; another with his whisperings to himself; a third with his clanking heels; a fourth with his wo-worn look."[6]

Masson's familiarity with the Reading Room continued during the ensuing decades, while he himself became one of the figures he had described, the biographer of Milton and thus "the conscientious writer of history." In 1857, when the new domed room was opened, seating capacity was more than doubled, so that an average of slightly over 400 people used the Reading Room each day.[7] (It was of course necessary to go in person to the Reading Room to consult the museum's materials, since, then as now, books could not be checked out and taken away.) There was more room for books as well. Antonio Panizzi, Keeper of the Department of Printed Books, brought pressure on publishers who had been evading their obligation to deposit with the museum a copy of every publication registered with the Stationer's Company of London; and he greatly increased the number of books obtained in this way.

The catalogue, of which Masson had complained in 1851, then consisted of large volumes of blank pages, upon which pages were pasted handwritten slips describing the books in the museum's collection. The system had some similarity to the quite flexible card catalogues familiar to American library users, as the slips could be unpasted and rearranged, and as new pages could be added to the volumes. The result was immensely bulky, however, as the museum's mountain of books grew higher. By 1875 the catalogue numbered over two thousand volumes. At the turn of the century something was done about it; the catalogue was printed, reducing its bulk while preserving essentially the same system; it is this collection of volumes which endured through the twentieth century, round and round the central portion of the Reading Room, trailing off into microform in preparation for the British Library's eventual flight to its new quarters on the Euston Road.

Like many of the basic reference works to be found on the Reading Room's open shelves, the room itself and the concept it represents— exhaustive collections, well catalogued, accessible to users—has become so familiar that we may be tempted to take it and its sister institutions, all the world's great libraries, for granted. It is worthwhile to stop and think what this new idea meant to Victorian scholars in general and to specialists in the new discipline of English literature in particular. To have at their fingertips material which would have taken years to track down in any other habitat made feasible the kind of investigation which resulted in many of the building blocks of English studies—just when the new subject needed them most.

Friends and Fiancées

Masson's literary endeavors provided him not only with professional recognition but with a social life as well. Unlike Henry Morley, who was active in the same profession at the same time but had a family to absorb any moments of leisure he might chance upon, Masson needed his evenings in company to balance the hours he spent at his desk. He found his companions to be lively, intelligent, often eccentric. Thackeray's portrait of London journalistic subculture in *Pendennis* (1850) was generally admired as a just one, and in fact his Captain Shandon, editing away while in debtor's prison and ordering up bottles of wine for his guests, is said to be based upon William Maginn, first editor of *Fraser's Magazine.* Other members of the circle were more sedate, giving dinner parties and musical evenings like other Victorians; but a keen interest in what was going on and a willingness to stand upon principle was characteristic of the majority of them.

In the early 1850s Masson's social acquaintance spread in a particularly compatible direction when he was introduced to Charles and Eliza Orme and their family. Among the Ormes' friends were many members of the literary and artistic group known as the Pre-Raphaelite Brotherhood, a movement devoted to resisting what they saw as the hackneyed conventions of their own time with a return to the ideals of Italian painting of the fourteenth and fifteenth centuries. Perhaps fortunately, the group seems to have had in fact little detailed knowledge of their chosen period, and in pursuit of their goal they achieved what has been increasingly recognized as a school of imaginative and original English art. The literary side of the brotherhood included the poet Coventry Patmore, who married Mrs. Orme's younger sister Emily Andrews. Among the many others whom Masson met in the Ormes' drawing room were Dante Gabriel Rossetti, brother of the poet Christina Rossetti and center of the Pre-Raphaelite movement; the painter

Holman Hunt, whose first Pre-Raphaelite painting, *Rienzi*, had been
accepted by the Royal Academy in 1849 and whose *The Light of the
World* in 1854 was to make him famous; and the sculptor Thomas
Wooler, who at that point in his career specialized in portrait medal-
lions and had won acclaim for his renditions of Wordsworth and Carlyle.

Masson's pleasure in his company included that of his hosts as
well as their guests, and in 1853 he married the eldest daughter, Emily
Rosaline Orme. For several years thereafter the couple lived with the
bride's parents, there being plenty of room in the house on Avenue
Road, near Regent's Park. Here the first of their four children was
born, and here, in a study set aside for his use, Masson wrote the first
volume of his biography of Milton.

University College

University College in 1852 was in one of its periodic searches for a
Professor of English, none up to this point having proved satisfactory.
Onlookers must have wondered if the new subject was ever going to
jell. As a candidate for the post, Masson was young, barely into his
thirties, but because of the institution's low-budget scale of operations
and consequent small salaries, young professors were the usual staple
of the academic deparments.

Masson also fit in very well with regard to principles. Since its
founding two decades before, University College had held deliberately
to a course distinct from that of Cambridge and Oxford, where cen-
turies-old ties with the Church of England had produced an environ-
ment both hostile to learning (in the sense of change and experiment)
and unfair to students excluded by the religious barriers—or so at least
University College thought while looking farther afield for its own
models. H. Hale Bellot's analysis of the educational backgrounds of
University College's original twenty-eight professors shows six as foreign
born and foreign educated, seven as having been born in England but
educated on the Continent or in the United States, six as Cambridge
products (none from Oxford), and twelve as veterans of the Scottish
universities.[8] These figures do not add up precisely because there is
some overlap—an education divided between Cambridge and Ger-

many, for example. Scotland in any case provided the largest single intellectual influence.

Not only were Masson's birth and education associated in University College's view with the free pursuit of knowledge, his career bore out this theme as well. His essays, many of them on literary topics befitting his new professorship, regularly appeared in journals associated with Scottish and liberal viewpoints. The *North British Review*, for example, had published Masson's comparison entitled *"Pendennis* and *Copperfield*, Thackery and Dickens,"* a substantial essay of some thirty pages, in May of 1851 and an even lengthier consideration of Milton's works in February of 1852.

During Masson's thirteen years at this post, the study of English at University College became a considerably more prominent part of the academic landscape. An important milestone was passed in 1859 when the University of London revised its degree requirements to include English language and literature as one of the language options, a matter described in a previous chapter in connection with Morley. The number of students attending English lectures then rose in a slow but steady fashion; by the time Morley succeeded to the chair, the income derived from their fees could more nearly keep a family in comfort—always assuming the professor could also pull together some outside lectures, bits and pieces of journalism, and moonlighting endeavors generally.

One of Masson's major outside projects was his editorship of *Macmillan's Magazine*, from its inauguration in 1859 until his relinquishing the helm, two years after his move to Edinburgh in 1867. In the course of superintending this monthly publication, Masson wrote a lengthy essay for almost every issue—sometimes political, sometimes literary—and of course devoted many hours to the odds and ends simply of getting the magazine out. *Macmillan's* carried work by F. D. Maurice, Harriet Martineau, Thomas Hughes, and Charles Kingsley; *Tom Brown at Oxford* and *Water Babies*, respectively the work of the last two authors named, were serialized in *Macmillan's* in the early 1860s.[9]

At University College, meanwhile, Masson's editorial visibility enhanced his growing reputation as a lecturer, and the college authorities no doubt congratulated themselves on having made a good choice. Such congratulatory moments in the groves of academe tend to have a predictable sequel. If a professor proves all that good, and if he is laboring for a pittance at the college which was alert enough to spot his potential, then someone else is likely to notice him and entice him away. Masson was noticed by the University of Edinburgh, whose Professor of Rhetoric and Belles Lettres, the poet and ballad collector William Edmonstoune Aytoun, had just died.

The appeal of this offer rested not entirely in the prospect of making more money, although for the father of a family this aspect was to be considered, but much more in the fact that Masson's heart was bound up in Scotland in general and in Edinburgh in particular. He could now consider his London career a success; he was an author and man of letters, a professor of distinction in a field he was helping to develop, and after all this he had a chance to come home.

Returning to Edinburgh

In many ways the city had not changed since Masson last lived there, almost twenty years before. The streets in Old Town still twisted themselves into mazes, while those in the newer eighteenth-century section to the north still joined their squares and crescents in a more geometrically decorous fashion; on Princes Street the new Walter Scott monument, the construction of which in 1844 Masson had probably observed as he went about his business for R. and W. Chambers, still startled the eye; and the ancient Castle on its pedestal of volcanic rock still loomed above all more temporary civic concerns. There was an increased air of busyness, however. The tide of mid-Victorian prosperity had reached Scotland. The railways, for example, affected not only commerce but daily life, as journeys which used to take days could be performed in hours. The remoter parts of the country were now less isolated from the capital, and students arriving at the University may have felt somewhat less as though they had passed irrevocably into another world.

The University buildings stood, as many of them still do, in the neighborhood of George Square. Edinburgh being a compact city, the Massons in their several movings about during the following thirty years—living first in Regent Terrace near Holyrood Palace, then among the Georgian vistas of Great King Street, and finally in Lockharton Gardens in the southwestern part of the city—remained in easy reach of the lecture halls.

By coincidence, the University of Edinburgh at the same time found a position for another prominent Scot living in London, Thomas Carlyle, (one of Masson's early benefactors) who became rector of the University. Unlike Masson at this point, Carlyle was at the end of his career. In his mid-sixties, ill, depressed by the death of his wife Jane (whom Masson remembered as the lively and intelligent hostess of the Carlyle home in Cheyne Walk), he lived for the most part in seclusion. In the 1870s he was to develop a tremor in his hands which made writing impossible. Nevertheless, he commanded respect, and his death in 1881 would be an occasion for civic mourning in Edinburgh and of special sorrow for Masson, whose book *Carlyle Personally and in His Writings* (1885) commemorates their friendship.

With Masson's arrival the University changed the title of the chair he had come to fill. Rather than Professor of Rhetoric and Belles Lettres, Masson became Professor of Rhetoric and English Literature. The change has a number of implications. The term *belles lettres*, though it does have to do with the study of literature, connotes aesthetic appeal, standards of taste, rather than the linguistic and historical continuum appropriate to the subject as Masson and many of his contemporaries saw it. In combination with the study of rhetoric, belles lettres tended to treat literature as a kind of window display, to be taken in snippets, an extract here and an epigram there, as illustrations for rhetorical techniques. Masson was to have a more systematic approach.

The University of Edinburgh's assumption that both rhetoric and literature could be dealt with in a single course is a familiar one, raising difficulties with which many English departments have coped and are still coping. The problem is that in this combination the rhetoric component almost inevitably seems to lose out. The teaching of rhetoric has built into it a negative twist. Neither students nor teachers, in large numbers at least, are drawn to a pursuit in which the chief activity seems to be finding out how wrong one is, or even, to put the matter in a more positive light, how much more effective one might become if one only did this or that. Literature, on the other hand, not only offers an immediate escape from this and other discomforts but achieves a more dramatic interest even in its drier aspects of historical periods, authors, and titles. A discipline with a strong historical dimension will often seem to have more going on, more that requires explanation; and its infringement upon other parts of the syllabus can become habitual. Masson's firm solution was to divide his course into distinct components, fencing rhetoric away from its competition, and to let the students know at all times exactly where they were. In this endeavor he may have been aided by the fact that rhetoric was at that time the more traditional study and was what the students were expecting.

The importance of English rhetoric to education in Scotland can be seen in the fact that Masson's chair had been established as far back as 1762. Rhetoric itself, of course, had been part of the curriculum since the University of Edinburgh's origins in the middle ages, but it was studied from the basis of Latin and Greek literature, as was the case all over Europe. The English language was from this perspective merely a local dialect without status or utility in the wider realms of civilization, and its advantages as a subject of rhetorical study were realized somewhat slowly. In this development a major impetus was the Reformation of the sixteenth century. Church services were thereafter conducted in English, and a good, well-argued sermon was highly valued. The Scottish church, relying less upon a set liturgy than did the Church of England, laid particular stress on the effective use of language in sermons, and in religious discussion and controversy generally; and such teaching was incorporated first into ministerial training, then into the more general degree of Master of Arts. (In England, the effective use of one's native tongue became in the post-Reformation period a much-taught subject at the so-called "dissenting academies" which did their best to educate those young men barred for religious reasons from Cambridge and Oxford. As in Scotland, the student body at these establishments was often composed of prospective ministers of Noncomformist churches; and the study of English rhetoric was pointed toward the writing of sermons.)

The earliest occupant of Masson's chair had been the well-known Hugh Blair, a clergyman and sermon writer and also the author of a treatise on the subject he now professed, *Lectures on Rhetoric and Belles Lettres*.[10] This work, based on a series of lectures by the political economist Adam Smith (whose inspiration Blair acknowledged in a somewhat inconspicuous manner), had gone into more than twenty editions, not counting abridgments, by Masson's time, and was still in use in both Britain and the United States as a standard textbook. Blair's work was more heavily weighted with general observations on the importance of style in conveying the good and the beautiful than with practical advice on a level accessible to students; but it seems to have raised the prestige of the subject.

The newfangled notion of adding literature to a course in rhetoric produced a variety of reactions. Masson's old friend of Aberdeen and London, Alexander Bain, now teaching at the University of Aberdeen, was against it, feeling that English literature had no place in the college curriculum. Bain was not against literature; he simply felt that writers and readers should be able to make contact with each other without need of professorial assistance, and in the *Fortnightly Review* of 1896 he enlarged his views:

> I hold that an English poet that has not of himself sufficient attraction to be read, understood, and relished, without the prelections of a University professor, is by that very fact a failure. He undertakes to charm the sense and fill the imagination of the ordinary reader, without more effort of study than is repaid on the post at the moment; his return for any labor expended on him is immediate or nothing. Any special difficulties ensuing from remoteness of age, from the wide scope of his imagery, or from any accidental defects of his composition, may be removed by his elegant and admiring commentator, to be redeemed by his irresistable charms in other respects. If we are to allow a coach in addition to the editor and the review critic, the popular evening lecturer is quite enough. The youthful pupil's forenoon hours are too precious for this kind of work . . . I could not vote to tax the nation for coaching *Hamlet* and *Macbeth*. . . . The English teacher's concern with the literature of the past is to extract from it everything that is of value for improving the diction of the pupils, and in that view the present, not the past, is his mainstay. [11]

To Masson, who respected his old friend but maintained his own priorities, the undergraduates' prime working hours were quite appropriately spent with *Hamlet* or *Macbeth*, even though their diction was not neglected either.

Masson on the Podium

During his thirty years' service to the University of Edinburgh, Masson taught essentially the same course to a total of over five thousand undergraduates, at the rate of between 150 and 200 each year. [12] The course took up both terms of a school year, could be taken at any time during a student's undergraduate career, and was divided into three parts described in the University *Calendar*.

Part one dealt with rhetoric in a theoretical way, with lectures on style, and a sorting out of all literature into a number of categories— "historical and descriptive literature," "expository or didactic literature," and so on. Part two, the relatively new study of English literary history, presented a chronological survey in which the writers from each period were described, with the important ones "reviewed more at large"; attention was paid to political and other connections with history in general; and, of course, students were given "a view of the main facts in the history and growth of the English language."[13]

All this might seem easily a year's worth, but there was more. Part three, "practical instruction in English composition," moved from the theoretical to the practical. Students wrote brief exercises in the classroom and turned in others, composed at more leisure, on assigned subjects. The *University Calendar* stipulated that an hour a week of class time was to be spent on this part of the course, and, to add a bit of zest, the Professor promised "prizes for merit in the Essays, in addition to the other Class-Prizes."[14]

Since the English course was a degree requirement, a professor would be dealing with matters students were sure to be asked about on their exams. Since Masson for much of his career was the only professor to give it, he naturally became a well-known figure. James Barrie, perhaps best known today as the author of *Peter Pan*, sat in Masson's classroom and has left a description of his experience. Masson, he remembers, spoke on his feet, pacing about and

> trying to tear the gas bracket from its socket. . . . It was when his mind groped for an image that he clutched the bracket. He seemed to tear his good things out of it. Silence overcame the class. Some were fascinated by the man; others trembled for the bracket. It shook, groaned, and yielded. Masson said another of the things that made his lectures literature; the crisis was passed; and everybody breathed again. . . . There were the inevitable students to whom literature is a trial, and sometimes they called attention to their sufferings by a scraping of the feet. Then the professor tried to fix his eyeglass on them, and when it worked properly they were transfixed. As

a rule, however, it required so many adjustments that by the time his eye took hold of it he had remembered that students were made so, and his indignation went. Then, with the light in his eye that some photographer ought to catch, he would hope that his lecture was not disturbing their conversation.[15]

Another former student, David Rorie, recalls one of Masson's composition assignments, an optional poetry competition on the subject of Edinburgh Castle. The Gilbert and Sullivan comic operas were popular at the time, and Rorie and a classmate, selecting as victim one of their number, "a humorless individual," concocted and sent in under his name a parody of "Tit-willow":

> High up on the top of a towering rock,
>   Is a castle, a castle, a castle.
> If you fell from that top it would give you a shock,
>   'Neath that castle, that castle, that castle,[16]

. . . and so on. Masson gave this effort a warm reception. After announcing the legitimate prizes he went on to praise it as "a squib, not without merit of its kind, which surprises me when I consider who is the author." The class shouted for the name. "I see no objection to stating it—it was Mr. X." Continues Rorie, "The victim rose in horror, to be at once pulled back into his seat," and as the class dismissed, "one could see him on the rostrum, denying, with excited gestures, the alleged paternity."[17]

Most of Masson's students seem to have approached their English course with a more consistent solemnity—with a kind of awe, in fact. The University archives preserve a number of their class notebooks. Some of these have been professionally bound, in cloth or even in calf, and obviously held an honored place in their owners' libraries throughout their post-University days. The handwriting is often beautiful—too beautiful, in some cases, to have been done as the lecture was actually in progress, complete as these pages are with diagrams neatly shaded and an occasional ornamental capital. The writers may have taken scratch notes in class and then recopied them in a more permanent form, a procedure which was probably a good way to review.

The notes themselves constitute a disappointment if one is seeking examples of the wit, flair, and timing which Barrie recalls in his memoir. Most of the students in fact seem to be following as best they can a speaker who is clearly traveling at his own speed rather than giving dictation in a deliberate manner; occasionally they drop a stitch and transcribe something Masson could not possibly have said. Attention often rests rather ponderously on the details of assignments. For a 2,000-word essay on "The Fool in *King Lear*," assigned in February of 1882, a student records, "What is wanted is not an abstract of *King Lear* but try to clutch the one character and study and explain Shakespeare's notion of the character and what is his function—what is his business in the play."[18] Efforts to prevent one's students from turning in a plot summary instead of an essay seem to go back a long way. With regard to this topic, incidentally, we might recall that the function of the Fool in *Lear* may have been seen as somewhat controversial. Nahum Tate's seventeenth-century rewriting of the play was only slowly being driven from the stage during the nineteenth century; in this version the Fool is omitted as extraneous to the action.

In the composition section of the course, Masson's hints on usage are often quite practical and aim at making the speaker or writer understood. In Scottish, for example, the Professor points out that the phrase "I don't mind" has the meaning of "I don't remember," while in English the same words mean "I don't care."[19] (One finds by reference to the *Oxford English Dictionary*, the M volume of which was not available to Masson or his students because it had not yet been published, that the Scottish form is the older.) With regard to the vexed question of *shall* and *will*—a distinction which greatly exercised the nineteenth century but which had been invented by a series of eighteenth-century grammarians frustrated by the inelegance of harboring two words with the same meaning—Masson is flexible enough to give the sources of the rules he cites and thus to imply that the rules are perhaps not carved in stone. "Dr. Alexander Adams, Rector of the High School," he says and the student duly writes, "gives the following rule concerning the use of 'shall' and 'will' in a Latin grammar, wherein he meant to teach Latin and English together, in 1793: 'Will,' in the first person singular or plural promises or threatens, while in the second or third person 'will' only foretells. 'Shall,' on the contrary, in the first person simply foretells, but in the second or third person promises, commands, or threatens. . . . This rule of Dr. Adams' is worth remembering; although it may seem a little hazy at first."[20] The rule also, unfortunately, tended to turn up on examinations, when one hopes that the haziness caused by an artificial distinction could be at least temporarily overcome; and it persists in various forms today, generating usage notes on "the expression of futurity" in the most up-to-date of dictionaries.

Literary history received thorough attention in Masson's class, where the students read not only outlines and summaries but as much of the primary material as could be worked in. Shakespeare and Milton were favorites in this regard. Not surprisingly, Masson's lectures often contained material which appears in his published essays and particularly in his edition of the poetical works of Milton (three volumes, 1874). The Shakespeare lectures reverse this pattern; instead of echoing works which Masson published during his lifetime, they comprise a book on their own, edited by Flora Masson several years after her father's death (*Shakespeare Personally*, 1914). These lectures, as the editor explains, underwent thirty years of revision as they were pronounced from the rostrum, and had pretty nearly achieved the form satisfactory to their author.

In neither his publications nor his lectures did Masson attempt to dictate any complex or insistent interpretive stance. He simply presented facts, arranged categories, made comparisons. He did, however, express his own interpretive preferences, and he encouraged his students to continue exploring on their own, urging them to read all of Shakespeare's plays and poems "individually, for their meanings," and continuing, according to one student's record, with a caution against an English form of insularity:

> This sort of study [close reading of texts] has been carried very far among the Germans, objections have been taken to this by Englishmen. The German philosophizing gets at the central ideas of the Writings. The English say that this is all nonsense but it is not. The best German commentary is Ulrici's "Shakespeare's Dramatic Art." The German method is a right one if well pursued. [21]

A *University of Edinburgh Examination*

The following examination (taken from the Calendar of 1883 but typical of any of Masson's thirty years at the helm) was given to all candidates for the Master of Arts degree of the previous year and represents what the University felt all its graduates should know in this field, regardless of any other specialty they might happen to cultivate. Three hours in length, its first hour was devoted to a single essay on any of the following subjects:

(a) The Grave-digging Scene in *Hamlet*
(b) Comparison of Milton's *Lycidas* with Tennyson's *In Memoriam*
(c) Carlyle's Estimate of Burns

The length of the essay was not stipulated, but candidates were warned that "Attention is expected to the expression and punctuation, as well as to the matter, of the Essay."

The remaining two hours were given to the questions below. The reader will notice a certain emphasis upon Scots writers, as in fact had already appeared in topic (c) above.

1. Explain and illustrate any two of the following phrases from the Lectures:
   (a) Addison's rule for avoiding Mixed Metaphor
   (b) Heterogeneous Sentence
   (c) Arnold's Definition of History Proper
   (d) The Synthetic Method in Exposition
   (e) Aristotle's Three Kinds of Oratory
   (f) Primary and Secondary Lyrics
2. Give a sketch of the origin and early history of the Arthurian legends.
3. To what extent, and in what manner, was Chaucer influenced (a) by French, (b) by Italian models? How far was the literature of the Elizabethan period affected by the same foreign influence?
4. Name *three* important English prose writers between 1300 and 1400, and *six* between 1580 and 1660, adding a brief descriptive note to each name.
5. Give approximately the dates, and name the chief works, of any six of the following writers, adding a short critical note with regard to each:—Marlow, Giles Fletcher, Jeremy Taylor, John Gower, Goldsmith, Henry Hallam, Gavin Douglas, Drummond of Hawthornden, Richardson, Massinger, Principal Robertson, Southey, Michael

Drayton, Gray, Sir Thomas Browne, Bishop Burnet, Cowper, Dryden.

6. What were the main varieties of English dialect in the fourteenth century, and how can they be distinguished from one another? What were the relations of those dialects (a) to the standard English of Chaucer and his successors, (b) to the Scotch of Barbour and his successors?

7. Annotate shortly as many as you can of the following passages:

   (a) "For neither were ye playing on the steep
      Where your old bards, the famous Druids, lie,
      Nor on the shaggy top of Mona high,
      Nor yet where Deva spreads her wizard stream."

   (b) "But that two-handed engine at the door
      Stands ready to smite once and smite no more."

   (c) "It faded on the crowing of the cock."

   (d) "Making night hideous, and we fools of nature
      So horridly to shake our disposition
      With thoughts beyond the reaches of our souls."

   (e) "Unhousel'd, disappointed, unanel'd."

   (f) "*Ros.* Truly, and I hold ambition of so light and airy a quality that it is but a shadow's shadow.
     Ham. Then are our beggars bodies, and our monarchs and outstretched heroes the beggars' shadows."

   (g) "O'erdoing Termagant; it out-herods Herod."

   (h) "The Danube to the Severn gave
      The darken'd heart that beat no more."

8. Give the metrical formulae, and the prosodic names, of the first seven of the following; and re-write No. *h* (which is a passage of blank verse printed as prose) in its proper blank verse form:

   (a) "Shakespeare described the sex in Desdemona."
   (b) "Youth's a stuff will not endure."
   (c) "Like the leaves of the forest when summer is green."
   (d) "Covered her slender shape with feathers of various plumage."
   (e) "Embalmed in the innermost shrine of her heart."
   (f) "His soul descended down into the Stygian realm."

(g) "Once to every man and nation comes the moment
    to decide."

(h) "For this he quits his home at day-spring, and no
    sooner doth the sun begin to strike him with a fire-
    like fervor than he lies down upon some rock, and
    there has breakfast with his dog."[22]

Understandably, Masson's students on completing this exam felt
they had acquired a considerable block of knowledge and could go out
into the world as educated citizens, with regard at least to the rhetoric
and literature of their native tongue. Present-day readers will presumably have found it at least a healthy bit of mental exercise.

Masson's Milton

A major fruit of Masson's lifelong interest in Milton, his edition of the
Poetical Works, went into numerous printings between 1874 and the
turn of the century. It was not the earliest scholarly edition of Milton;
Milton had been in fact the first English author to receive the modern
type of editorial attention, the work in question being Patrick Hume's
1695 *Annotations of Paradise Lost*, consisting of 321 folio pages.[23]
Hume was Scottish, though living in London, and his substantial *Annotations*, appearing not quite three decades after *Paradise Lost* itself,
was devoted to explanations of the classical and biblical allusions.
   The annotative approach to Milton is a necessary as well as an
irresistible one. The surface of the poetry is so deceptively simple, the
allusions so resonantly complex. Two eighteenth-century editors had
also left annotated editions, Thomas Newton's *Paradise Lost* in 1749
and Thomas Warton's *Minor Poems* in 1785, but Masson's work was
the first really weighty effort of the nineteenth century. It was welcomed
for that reason and also because Masson was the first to relate philology
in its new scientific form to Milton's poetry. His introductory "General
Essay on Milton's English," as well as many of the individual annotations, deals systematically with vocabulary and usage. The effect is
that the reader begins to feel that the state of philological art is finally
catching up with Milton; Milton had to wait a long time. On the well-
worn paths of allusions and references, Masson is often indebted to his
predecessors.

The scholarly work for which Masson is most frequently remembered, his biography of Milton, disconcerted his contemporaries as well as his later readers by including so much historical background that Milton himself sometimes disappears in the melee. The trend of biographical writing has since swung toward the tidier, single-focus effect, while Masson's six volumes, appearing between 1859 and 1880 and followed in 1894 by the index, seem by contrast to ramble all over the seventeenth century.

This negative impression can perhaps be countered by reading the full title: *The Life of John Milton, Narrated in Connexion with the Political, Ecclesiastical, and Literary History of His Time.* "It is intended that the title of this Work should indicate its character," the author states firmly in his opening volume, adding that he "has not deemed it unfit to allow the forms of Biography to overflow those of History."[24] If Masson did what he did on purpose, it seems unfair to judge the results by different standards. His deliberate juxtaposition of biography with history is demonstrated by the arrangement of the tables of contents. In volume two, for example, we see the following: "November 1640—August 1642. History: First two-and-twenty Months of the Long Parliament. Biography: Milton in Aldersgate Street; His Anti–Episcopal Pamphlets."

Masson's use of documents is exhaustive. We have, for example, detailed lists with thumbnail biographies of all the members of a given Parliament; all the officers of Cromwell's army. Documents having to do with local taxes provide Masson with a room-by-room description of the house occupied by Mary Powell, Milton's seventeen-year-old bride, and her parents; and Masson gives this and other close-up information while presenting a meticulous line up of the possible motivations, inferences, and hypothetical explanations of the mysterious sequence of events which, under whatever circumstances they may have begun, led eventually to the *Divorce Tracts.*

Since Carlyle had had a considerable influence upon the writing of history generally and upon Masson's journalistic career in particular, it is not surprising to find some similarity between the styles of the two. But Masson is more concerned than Carlyle with catalogues of fact, and his voice in general is calmer. The similarities are most noticeable when a historical event provides Masson with a Carlyle-esque moment—the execution of Charles I, for example. Here we have much vivid description—what clothes the monarch put on that morning, what friends visited him before the journey to the block—but the atmosphere is almost tranquil in comparison to similar scenes from *The French Revolution.* Masson's book, like English history itself, seems usually more deliberative than impulsive.

A final reason for the occasional dissatisfaction which present-day readers may find in the *Life* stems, quite possibly, from the subject himself. Milton lived a divided existence, torn between art and duty, inner preference and outer principle; and the events of his life scheduled themselves into a sequence the transitions of which are abrupt. Quite suddenly his party is defeated, the Royalists restored, enemy retribution avoided, Milton blind but still walking about in his garden; all he had to do was write *Paradise Lost,* or dictate it rather. Thus in Masson's biography, *Paradise Lost* becomes almost an anticlimax, and the reader feels left behind. The subject of the book has left the stage, entering a realm of art into which the fact-bound biography cannot easily follow.

None of this was Milton's fault, or Masson's either, and the unevenness of the book when viewed as a panorama tends to disappear in the closer-up views. Here its interest and usefulness remain. One appreciates not only the facts, which have supplied generations of scholars busily weaving their own interpretations of Milton's life and works, but also Masson's attitude about the facts. He presents them, he speculates in a logical fashion about their implications, but he does not force his own preferences rigidly. An air of objectivity prevails. In the words of the *Cambridge History of English Literature,* the *Life* was "worked up and supplemented by Masson with heroic diligence, with lavish provision of commentary and without that undue expatiation into 'may-have-beens' and 'probablys' and 'perhapses' which, despite the temptation to it which exists in some cases, is irritating to the critically minded and dangerously misleading to the uncritical." This comment cannot be said to be wholly unbiased, for it happens to have been written by George Saintsbury, Masson's successor at the University of Edinburgh; but it describes a consistently valid aspect of Masson's work.

Into the Next Century

On retiring from his professorial duties in 1895, Masson spent the next twelve years talking to friends, walking the streets of Edinburgh as a known and respected figure (he was said to come to resemble more and more his late friend Carlyle), and combatting the Scottish winters with blazing parlor fires—or such is the impression given by Flora Masson.[25] The University had marked his retirement with an assortment of honors, and the Edinburgh Ladies' Educational Association, whose campaign for the University degree (successful in 1892) he had energetically supported, in 1897 gave their new women's residence in George Square the name of Masson Hall. (There is still a residential Masson Hall, now on South Lauder Road; the original one stood on the side of George Square now occupied by the new University buildings of the 1960s.) An official marble bust, presented by subscription to the University of Edinburgh, was carved by J. P. Macgillivray; an official oil portrait, presented by the artist to the National Portrait Gallery in Edinburgh, was painted by Sir George Reid. Masson died in October of 1897, aged eighty-five, and was buried not far from the University, in the Grange Cemetery.

At this point, we might pause for a brief look forward and backward. English studies through the time of Masson have clearly come a long way. As a respectable discipline, a practical discipline, a discipline rather paradoxically contributing to the students' perception of the beauty and grace of life, English was by the turn of the century accepted as a solid component of education.

From the standpoint, however, of England's traditional nuclei of higher learning, the universities of Oxford and Cambridge, English studies had been developed by pretty much a bunch of outsiders. University College and the other University of London institutions had after all set themselves up deliberately to purvey education according to other than the established patterns. America was doomed to newness; with territory to fill in every sense, she might as well experiment with the untried. Scotland had a long tradition of being unimpressed by English tradition. In short, Oxford and Cambridge were not likely to feel they must hurry and admit English language and literature to their degree programs because all these other schools had done so; on the contrary, they may have regarded English with an even deeper suspicion because of its acceptance elsewhere. The shift in attitude came in stages, and some of the controversy was energetic. It seems unfair that, once the shift had taken place, Oxford and Cambridge respectively achieved a preeminence in English studies just as they had smugly assumed they would. In fact, we do not have to see it that way. English language and literature programs at the newer institutions all over England, in Scotland, in America, and for that matter throughout the English-speaking world did not go down in quality just because Cambridge and Oxford had entered the field. But it is undeniable that the traditional universities wielded a certain prestige, and that a historical view of English studies tends to see some events accompanying this development as milestones. We will enter this world with the career of Professor Skeat.

5

Walter William Skeat (1835–1912), Cambridge, and English Philology

Professors Child and Masson entered upon their scholarly careers through their own efforts, pulling themselves up by the bootstraps; Professor Morley had been given an education by his family, but as he had been launched into the wrong field, he had to climb out of the one and into the other. Walter William Skeat differs from all three in that he walked contentedly in the paths set before him, often followed the advice of his family and friends when faced with a choice, and lived his life very quietly. He was not a dynamic lecturer, did not shine as a public figure or rush about supporting causes. He would, in fact, seem an unlikely person to establish the study of English language and literature at Cambridge University, an institution which regarded innovations with distaste but which, once it had given in and accepted them, did so with a weighty commitment to quality, with a magnetic attraction for good instructors, with, in short, an immediate conferring of status upon the newly accepted discipline. That Skeat did bring about this change is a tribute to his powers of quiet perserverance.

Skeat's father was an architect and thus a member of a profession identified in Victorian times with moderation and middle-class respectability, rather than with the more startling forms of creativity later to spring up with the twentieth-century's architectural movements. Family members were also quite matter-of-factly Church of England, a circumstance that affected their choices of schools and careers in that more doors were open. Skeat was born in London, in Mount Street near Hyde Park; when he was two years old his family moved to Perry Hill, Sydenham, south of the Thames, now part of urban London but then in the countryside. Skeat recalls these years from a philological standpoint. In an autobiographical sketch, he mentions his childhood travels and family visits:

It was then that I acquired, by help of various opportunities, some acquaintance with the dialects of West Kent, London, and Essex. But the speech which became most familiar to me was that of South Shropshire, where I had many relatives. My mother once knew the dialect well.[1]

Of the several schools Skeat attended as a child, two have a bearing on his later interests. At King's College School in the Strand (which functioned as a preparatory school for nearby King's College), Skeat's instructor was the Reverend Oswald Cockayne, one of the most highly regarded Anglo-Saxon scholars of his time. Cockayne taught Latin and Greek in the school, Anglo-Saxon not being part of the curriculum; but he may have served as a role model. Another part of his influence was quite direct, having to do with principles and methods. In Skeat's words, "He was an excellent and painstaking teacher, and it was, I believe, from him that I imbibed the notion of what is known as scholarship." They were later to become personal friends.

Another school, this one situated in Highgate in northern London, introduced Skeat more or less accidentally to English literature:

[I]t was customary to give us occasionally scraps of it [English poetry], on which to exercise our skill by translating them into Greek and Latin verse. Probably it is by the same curious and circuitous course that boys still have English authors brought under their notice. However this may be, it is certain that no portion of our literature was ever explained to me at any of my five schools. It was then considered as a thing altogether apart from our ordinary curriculum, and only to be seriously regarded when in the privacy of our own homes during holidays. And what an astonishing fact this now seems to me to be! If we really possess, as many think, one of the finest literatures in the world, why are not boys informed of its value, and why are they not shown how to approach it with profit to themselves?[2]

It might be observed, incidentally, that Skeat's reference to "boys" does not necessarily imply that girls at this period were being taught great swatches of English literature and that Skeat intends to point out the difference. Skeat is merely using "boys," from force of habit, to mean the younger portions of the educable populace.

His childhood interest in English literature awakened, Skeat browsed on his own in the school library, which contained "a glorious copy of Spenser." At sixteen, he received as a school prize a copy of Shakespeare's works, of which edition (Steevens and Malone) he remembers that "the glossary, of course, has no references, but it was an amusement to supply them for myself."

This last observation, though undeniably of the sort that can rouse some lovers of literature to an antiphilological fury, is here made by Skeat in perfect innocence. He would have no idea why anyone might look askance at it. In his own view, he was not murdering to dissect; and the assumption that an enthusiasm for words is incompatible with an enthusiasm for the literature in which the words are used was one with which he took issue:

> It will thus be seen that, in my case, a love of our splendid literature was early formed, and at no time required any external stimulus. But this does not explain how I came to take a special delight in the linguistic and philological side of it, whilst revelling in its appeal to the imagination. Some are tempted to suppose that a critical examination of language is likely to interfere with the romantic element. I have never found it so in any appreciable degree; and I sometimes suspect that those who decry philology want to make us believe, with the fox, that the grapes are sour. Why are we to be debarred from examining a poet's language because his words are sweet and his descriptions entrancing? That is only one more reason for weighing every word that he uses.[3]

Skeat's love for philology needed no external stimulus either, but in a sense he did have one that in that so few dependable reference works were in existence—dictionaries, for example, that form of basic tool which we now take blithely for granted, reaching for a dictionary as we might reach for a glass of water. When Skeat reached for a dictionary, he often found it either nonexistent or full of holes. He wished to know, of course, not only a word's current meaning but its history and pedigree, and the flimsy efforts—creative, one might say— he frequently encountered in this line drove him to heights of exasperation. In this way a sense of mission pervaded the lives of Skeat and his philological colleagues—a mission which, ironically, they fulfilled so well that later generations now have difficulty imagining the need for it.

Cambridge in the 1850s

In 1854, when Skeat became an undergraduate, Cambridge had no Department of English, a fact for which we have been prepared; but it had no other departments either. The transmission of knowledge at the traditional English universities was not organized in this way. Even mathematics and classical languages, which Cambridge emphasized and upon which undergraduates were examined for their degrees, had no university departments, none of the familiar hierarchy of a chairman at the top of the pyramid and a broadening base of professors, assistants, and so on, coherently selected for teaching and research in their individual specialties. This arrangement, which like so many features of academic life derives from Germany, became naturalized in America after it was imported in the nineteenth century; many of the newer English institutions, seeking as did University College for a variety of models, chose to follow the German one in this regard. But in both Cambridge and Oxford, most of the actual teaching was done within the individual colleges which collectively made up the University.

Cambridge did have on its books a few University Professors, men whose responsibilities lay toward the whole university rather than toward any one of its component colleges. These University professorships had come about through what might be seen as a fairly haphazard process. The individual chairs had been founded over the centuries by individual benefactors, each of whom had set up an endowment for the teaching of some subject which the benefactor happened to think important. In 1854, for example, when Skeat became an undergraduate, the Univeristy had twenty or so professors (there was some overlap with the category of University Preachers), holding chairs founded between 1502 and 1819 in such subjects as divinity, civil law, mathematics, Greek, Hebrew, chemistry, geology, Arabic, and so on. There was no mechanism allowing the University to shake up and streamline the whole kaboodle, to reorganize the categories if necessary, to add subjects if needed, and to prune out any that had withered away. A chair, once established, remained; a new chair, however badly needed, had to wait for a benefactor to emerge and think of it.

The professors' salaries depended upon the size of the endowment of their respective chairs, from the interest of which they were paid, although in a few cases inflation over the centuries had reduced the buying power of a stipend so much that the University augmented it by amounts ranging from one hundred to four hundred pounds annually. In other cases, depending upon the investments that had been made, the stipend had over the years become worth more rather than less. While the founder of a chair would give the money, specify the subject, and perhaps make other stipulations—requiring, for instance, a certain number of lectures a year—the choice of the man to fill the chair would be made by the University authorities. These choices were in turn influenced by the alumni. Since Oxford and Cambridge men tended more or less to run the country, holding decided opinions and enjoying considerable self-confidence in expressing them, the naming of a professor to a University chair often became a matter of public concern, demonstrated by letters in the *Times* and controversial essays in the quarterlies.

In 1854, Skeat entered not so much the University of Cambridge as Christ's College. A prospective undergraduate applied to and was accepted or rejected by an individual college, not the University as a whole. From the undergraduate's perspective, the University was merely the vague entity which administered examinations and granted degrees.

Christ's was one of seventeen colleges then under the University's corporate supervision. Each was a discrete entity, with its own history and traditions, and each, with its buildings grouped usually in a pattern of courtyards, presented as they do today a curiously defensive aspect, as if prepared to withstand an invasion from the college across the street. They had of course been there for centuries. Peterhouse is usually accepted as the oldest Cambridge college, founded in 1284, while five others date from the fourteenth century. Chist's might consider itself a relative newcomer, having been established as late as 1505. There were, however, five colleges dating from later in the sixteenth century, their founders in effect redistributing some of the wealth they had gained after the dissolution of the monasteries. Trinity College, for example, was founded by Henry VIII himself.

Some of the colleges, those which had been endowed with the right sums at the right time and whose investments had been carefully looked after, were by the nineteenth century enormously wealthy. Thus isolated from dependence upon the outside, they had in a sense become little worlds to themselves. The instructors attached to each college—fellows, tutors, dons, lecturers—titles which overlap in actual usage but which convey the familiar impression of a gowned and learned gentleman drifting through the cloisters, were chosen by the colleges themselves, often from among their own graduates. Their stipends were paid from the college's funds and were only minimally, if at all, connected with any fees which might be paid by the undergraduates.

Unlike the University Professors, who lectured but who were not required to give tests, mark papers, assign grades, or otherwise follow the progress of their hearers, the college tutors were responsible for the academic growth of the students enrolled in their college. Ordinarily each undergraduate was assigned a tutor, whom he visited at appointed times to be given reading lists, recommendations of lectures to attend, assignments in the form of essays on given topics, or perhaps encouragement to try for one of the college prizes in various subjects.

Since fees paid by students were not a significant item in the salaries earned by either the University Professors or the college tutors, we might pause to look for a moment at the student's side of the financial picture: What did he pay for his education? The answer is, not much, relatively speaking, allowing for a large number of options. In Skeat's time, an undergraduate could get by in reasonable comfort for as little as £61, the average expenditure suggested by the *University Calendar* for 1854. This sum allowed for a few small university fees, £10 for tuition, and £5 for laundry. Room charges occupied a quite flexible scale, ranging from £4 to £30 with most students paying about £10. (Rooms in college, one might add, were often on the spartan side by present-day standards, even though a servant was usually supplied to make the fire.) Meals would cost about £20. Most of these expenses could be managed more cheaply if necessary, and various types of financial aid were available. Thus a young man could gain access to libraries, instruction, and academic opportunity generally for the equivalent in late twentieth-century dollars of about $3,000—nothing to sneeze at, but not exactly ruinous either—provided, of course, he were of the correct social class, as demonstrated by his religion. The *Calendar* is explicit: "The University confers no degree whatever, unless the Candidate has previously subscribed a declaration that he is *bona fide* a member of the Church of England, as by law established."[4] (Cambridge was less rigid than Oxford on this point. At Oxford one needed to declare one's correct faith before one could matriculate; at

Cambridge one could in theory go through an undergraduate career and then leave without the degree. Few people did so, however.[5] Religious requirements at both Oxford and Cambridge were removed by the end of the century.)

An extravagant undergraduate might, of course, manage to spend a great deal more than average; as those who were wealthy enough to do so naturally achieved a high degree of visibility, the traditional picture of nineteenth-century Cambridge and Oxford as a panorama of champagne picnics and elegant clothes is a true even if not a typical one. For many, the goal of university life was simply to make friends, learn the mores of the upper middle class into which they had been born, and generally sift themselves out into patterns of expectations and loyalties which would be useful later in life. England was a small society, especially at the top. During this process, some acquaintance with the traditional academic disciplines was assumed to be beneficial. One read for one's final examinations with greater or less dedication, and passed them more or less well; the results were announced in categorical lists, so that one knew at once if one had taken a good degree. An undergraduate might even fail his examinations and be "sent down" with no degree at all, without, usually, anything very terrible happening. One could not very well be expelled from the upper middle class; some niche in life would be found for one, and this minor point in one's past history would be forgotten.

During the later half of the nineteenth century, both Oxford and Cambridge brought themselves by slow stages into alignment with reformists' views, even eventually welcoming women as well as nonmembers of the Church of England. The curriculum was limbered up and made more responsive to national needs. But even with its obvious faults, the older system in which the choice of studies was limited to those which the colleges felt personally inclined to supervise cannot be said to have been entirely bad. Students may have found a narrow range in the official curriculum, but nothing prevented their following their own interests outside it, and many did so with a zeal that might have been weaker had every effort on their part been measured out for academic credit. Instructors trapped in a rut could escape to fields of their own choice in their leisure time, and it is possible that the advancement of learning benefited from their having so much choice as well as so much leisure. Certainly the nineteenth century saw a great deal of work in philology, both classical and Germanic, being done by Oxford and Cambridge dons outside their assigned duties.

Skeat As Undergraduate and As Country Curate

Skeat chose Christ's College, as he explains in the autobiographical sketch quoted above, chiefly because of its size. He wanted a college "large enough for forming acquaintances"—large enough, that is, presumably, for exercising some choice in one's acquaintances—but not so large as to overwhelm him with competition. Christ's proved sufficient in both respects, as Skeat valued his friends there and also achieved considerable scholastic recognition.

Christ's College was much the same, as far as appearance and ambiance are concerned, in Skeat's day as in ours—although it lacked, naturally, the curious tier of modern buildings added to the college's farther reaches in the twentieth century. The gardens were as green, the courtyards as trim, as they had been when Milton was enrolled there. Christ's College misses some picturesque potential through its not being located on the Cam and thus having access to neither punts nor willow trees, but aside from this disadvantage it is as handsome a college as any in Cambridge.

Here Skeat followed the traditional curriculum quite happily. In mathematics he did particularly well and eventually placed high in the list of degree candidates in that subject. He also had a natural turn for languages, and, as he intended to go into the Church, he was interested in theology. English literature he tended to regard as a private indulgence. As he tells us:

> [T]hroughout my college life, classics, mathematics, and theology were my more serious studies, whilst Chaucer, and Spenser, and Shakespeare were an unfailing resource in many an hour of leisure. My future was, as I then supposed, to be spent in the obscurity of a country curacy, and our great writers could be safely depended upon for affording excellent companionship on a rainy day.[6]

Upon entering Christ's, Skeat found himself one of eighty-seven undergraduate members; the following year he was named a college scholar, an honor which carried a small stipend. During all three years of his undergraduate residency, Skeat took first prize among his peers in the college's annual class examinations. The prizes were books, in value three guineas a year. By way of variety, he took in his second year one of the prizes in "the Greek testament and the doctrines and formularies of the Church of England."

On completing his degree, Skeat then read for holy orders, which he took in 1860. In the same year he married Miss Bertha Jones of Lewisham—at that time a small village, like Sydenham and quite close to it, on the Ravensbourne River—and obtained a curacy in East Dereham, Norfolk. Skeat was then only twenty-five, rather young for marriage by Victorian standards. However, his prospects, if not lavish, were steady. Curates as a class were notoriously underpaid; a curate's salary derived not from any sort of church fund or from the tithes of the parish he served, but simply from the pocket of the rector whose assistant he had become. (The rector's pockets were filled from a variety of sources, usually including some part of the parishioners' tithes, and as there were rich parishes and poor parishes a rector's income could vary considerably.) It was, however, generally assumed of a young curate just starting out that better things would follow, that he would move on to a better paid curacy and would eventually himself become rector of a parish. This last step generally involved buying the living, a perfectly legal and aboveboard transaction. The cost might be heavy but the investment would usually prove worthwhile. The financial aspect of the clerical life is mentioned here only for a sense of perspective and not to imply that people customarily went into the Church of England for the money. There were better ways to make a fortune. Certainly Skeat, like many of his fellow clergymen, was drawn to this career for the opportunities it offered of a quiet and useful life.

The young couple passed two years in East Dereham, where Skeat, following up his extracurricular interests as he had planned to do, gave a lecture to all who cared to attend "On the Origin and Progess of the English Language," which effort, he says, was received with favor. In it he emphasized the importance of Anglo-Saxon grammar and vocabulary as an influence on English—a fairly novel idea at the time, as the romance languages had received more attention by way of ancestral roots. The lecture was later published as a pamphlet. Skeat and his family (eventually to include five children) then moved on to a curacy in Godalming, Surrey, packing up, one imagines, the young curate's increasing library of philological works. Godalming, near Guildford, was famous for its scenery, and the parish church contained an item which made Skeat feel at home—a memorial tablet to Owen Manning, editor of Lye's *Anglo-Saxon Dictionary* in 1772.

At Godalming a misfortune befell Skeat which had the effect of changing his life:

The neighborhood was beautiful, but the climate proved unsuitable; and at last an alarming attack, of a diptheritic character, totally unfitted me for clerical work and rendered a long rest absolutely necessary; and I thus found myself, in the end of 1863, at the age of twenty eight, in the desolate condition of finding my chosen career brought to a sudden end, without any idea as to my future course, and even without much prospect of ever again rendering any help to my fellow creatures, which (I can truly say) has always been my object as regards this present world.[7]

At this unexpected turning, Christ's College came to the rescue; and after Skeat had spent some months in the idleness insisted upon by his physicians, he was appointed to a lectureship in mathematics.

Philology in the Ascendant

For someone in need of rest, and in particular someone whose throat had been under bacilli attack, teaching might seem the least likely of careers. One imagines a harried figure rushing through hallways, in and out of classrooms full of chalk dust, lecturing for hours, drawing sines and cosines on the blackboard, and then rushing out again with stacks of exercises to be corrected. The answer, of course, is that functioning as a mathematical lecturer at Cambridge was nothing like this at all. The University was under no obligation to provide the largest number of students possible with the best training possible, at the least expense possible—the necessity which hangs over many parts of the groves of academe and which finds expression frequently in very large lecture classes. All that Christ's College had to do was to find a bit of slack in its endowment income to pay a modest but sufficient stipend to the Reverend Skeat. His duties were essentially a matter of being available to any of the College's undergraduates who felt they could use some help; as he put it, "I occasionally took a few pupils; but this left me a good deal of leisure time."

Casting about for a focal point for his life, Skeat made inquiries as to what fields might already be taken and found there was indeed a vacancy, in the way of personal if not of official pursuits:

I could not find that anyone in Cambridge had any very

accurate or extensive knowledge of Anglo-Saxon; and the idea occurred to me that, as it was obviously a useful study and in a fair way of becoming one of considerable importance, it would be a good plan to take up the subject.[8]

As he got his Anglo-Saxon studies under way, Skeat found himself interested as well in Middle English, and in this his timing was fortunate. By this point, in the mid-1860s, scholars were beginning to converge upon Middle English and some valuable works had just appeared. One of these, Richard Morris's *Specimens of Early English*, so impressed Skeat that he sat down and made a glossarial index for it. He sent his contribution to Morris, who was impressed in turn, and in the next edition (1871) Skeat's name appears with Morris's on the title page. The collaboration continued throughout several augmented editions until by the 1880s, specimens had been collected covering the era from 1150 to 1579.

In the meantime, Skeat had attracted the attention of F. J. Furnivall, ever on the alert for editors for his newly formed Early English Text Society. In 1865 Furnivall persuaded Skeat to undertake the editorship of *Lancelot of the Laik*, a fifteenth-century narrative poem which had been published in 1839 by the Maitland Club but which now, in Furnivall's opinion, needed reediting for the wider readership which the E.E.T.S. would give it. The one manuscript of the poem, Furnivall pointed out, was conveniently at Skeat's hand in the Cambridge University Library, and Skeat had only to check it against the Maitland Club edition. Skeat expressed doubts of his ability to read a medieval Scottish manuscript; Furnivall, to whom objections of this sort were negligible, replied that he could learn. Skeat's memories of this early project are worth quoting from the same autobiographical sketch which has done us so much service already. Skeat may exaggerate his own ignorance out of modesty, but he evokes the flavor of scholarly life in the pioneer days of the new subject, when one learned by doing.

My first inspection of the manuscript was not reassuring; in fact, anyone who can thoroughly master a Scottish manuscript of the end of the fifteenth century is in a fair position to be not easily daunted by manuscripts of an earlier date. But there was a teacher at hand such as few men ever had. To this day I can remember the smile of amused satisfaction with which the manuscript was brought out to me by our justly celebrated librarian, Henry Bradshaw by name, of King's College. I must suspect that he thought he had extinguished me; indeed, after puzzling over the first page for a couple of hours, I was not conscious of having advanced beyond some twenty lines; and so retreated for that time. But as I gradually gained the courage to maintain that, if the manuscript was right, the printed copy was sometimes wrong, Bradshaw became interested, authoritatively confirmed all my emendations, and never failed to give me his most valuable aid.[9]

Bradshaw, a distinguished scholar as well as an industrious librarian, must presumably have escaped Furnivall's editorial dragnet by pleading the pressure of other work. He discovered lost or unrecorded manuscripts in the Cambridge library and elsewhere, worked out theories on the relationships of Chaucerian fragments, compiled numerous catalogues and other bibliographical works, and was active in the Cambridge Antiquarian Society.

The discrepancy Skeat mentions between the Maitland Club edition of *Lancelot of the Laik* and the manuscript provided the young editor with a dramatic entrance into the ranks of early English scholarship. The Maitland Club edition, as Skeat's discoveries suggested, had beem made from a faulty transcript which had been checked against the original badly or not at all. The resulting ripples in the scholarly world were to the credit of the Early English Text Society, showing that this body took its mission seriously and aimed at accuracy. Furnivall promptly rewarded Skeat by talking him into a much more complex task, one which occupied him, although it shared his desk with many other projects in progress, for the next twenty years.

This undertaking, Skeat's edition of the fourteenth-century allegorical poem *Piers Plowman*, was published in several interim stages by the E.E.T.S. and finally by the Oxford University Press in 1886. It contrasts with his initial effort in a number of ways. *Lancelot of the Laik* existed in only one manuscript copy, which copy then becomes rather reassuringly the sole reality as far as the editor's job is concerned. The manuscript and the literary work are the same. A work of which more than one manuscript has survived enters a realm of considerably greater complexitiy. The editor, instead of treating his unique copy as a fait accompli regardless of the errors he might suspect it of containing, now has a choice, and the author's intentions may seem to disappear into a maze. A medieval manuscript was copied and sent on its way, time after time, the copies to be themselves copied, fanning out in all directions while errors multiplied and civilization awaited the invention of the printing press; the author, having meanwhile changed his mind and revised his work entirely, had no way of recalling the earlier versions. They just kept going. The fact that these tangles can be sorted out at all is a tribute to the versatility and flexibility of the human mind. In the nineteenth century scholars made great strides in detective work of this sort, focusing especially on the works of Chaucer; Furnivall's Chaucer Society concerned itself with the chronology of the manuscripts and published works by Furnivall, John Koch, and J. S. P. Tatlock which contributed pieces to the puzzle. [10]

In the case of *Piers Plowman*, a lengthy dream vision and satire the author of which Skeat lists as William Langland (although this identification has been a matter of speculation before and since), the scholar faces a formidable task. The author composed several distinct versions of the poem; Skeat was able to demonstrate that the number of versions is in fact three, not two as had previously been supposed. Each version has its own family of manuscripts, one scribe copying the text of another, while errors and oddities accumulate. Some forty-five manuscripts, complete or partial, survived to form the basis for the edition Skeat eventually produced. Here the three versions appear as parallel texts, page by page, backed up by notes and philological apparatus. The volumes still hold a proud place on library shelves.

During the years occupied by this endeavor, Skeat of course worked on many other things as well. For the E.E.T.S., Skeat edited some twenty volumes, although the tabulation is a difficult one because there were so many projects he had a hand in. With an introduction here and a glossary there, it is hard to know where to draw the line, while the volume-by-volume issue of works in progress also complicates the tally. [11] Other works were published by various dialect societies (including the English Dialect Society, which Skeat founded himself), both the Oxford and Cambridge university presses, and, from time to time, commercial publishers. Skeat sometimes received payment for these last, particularly for texts which were used in schools and which sold in fairly large numbers, but the bulk of his scholarly work was done for love rather than money.

In this last nonprofit category were numerous glossaries and dictionaries, among which several were conceived as aids to the Philological Society's *Oxford English Dictionary*, then in progress. (Skeat at one point took a direct part in this mammoth undertaking, compiling a section from *Ra* to *Re*; but his other commitments proved less flexible than he had thought they would be.) Among Skeat's many editions of medieval poetry are *Richard the Redeless*, *William of Palerne* (the world's most charming werewolf story), *The Romance of Alexander and Dindimus*, *The Wars of Alexander*, and, in a special category of influence and usefulness, his many editions of Chaucer. The *Complete Works* in seven volumes (1894–97), for several generations *the* Chaucer, formed a point of reference for the twentieth-century's brisk activity in Chaucer studies.

Prizes and Place Names

Throughout this editorial fervor, Skeat continued to fulfill his duties at Christ's College and to expand them in the direction of his own preferences. The 1866 *University Calendar*, a year after Skeat arrived wearing a mathematical hat, lists him as "Lecturer in Mathematics and the English Language"—a sign that the thirty-one-year-old instructor was on the lookout for undergraduates with an interest in the new subject and did his best to guide them in the right paths. In the same year, Skeat gave a hundred pounds of his own money to establish an annual prize for the Christ's College student writing the best examination in English language and literature. This examination was neither a college nor a University affair, but one Skeat made out himself. Subjects were announced in advance; a typical list includes *The Tempest*, *Richard II*, Chaucer's *Knight's Tale*, Milton's *Areopagitica*, Bacon's *Essays*, and Sidney's *Defense of Poetry*. Prospective candidates might presumably be well advised to prepare by attending Skeat's lectures. This combination of lectures, examination, and prize (the year's interest on the hundred pounds), with publicity for the winner as well, was a quite ingenious method for getting an academic study under way in the guise of an extracurricular hobby and is similar to the strategy used by the E.E.T.S. at about the same time.

In connection with Skeat's prize-founding activity, we might note that he performed a similar act in 1888 out of simple admiration, donating a hundred pounds toward a prize to be given in memory of Charles Darwin, who had been a Christ's College man in the 1830s— before Skeat's time but still a part of his era. An affinity between Darwin's evolutionary hypotheses and the kind of patterns drawn by the philologists is not hard to imagine, as both species of scholars were aware of the importance of the past and saw the varying processes which they studied as parts of a lengthy continuum. Skeat's interest in the history of place names might serve as an example. His investigations resulted in a series of county-by-county studies (Bedfordshire, Berkshire, Cambridgeshire, Hertfortshire, Huntingdonshire, and Suffolk). Arranged systematically by suffixes and prefixes, and going back to the Domesday Book (the eleventh-century survey of England made by William the Conqueror) and other authorities for the earliest spellings, these small books shed a considerable etymological light.

Yet another affinity, and a strong one, connecting the philologists and their more tangibly scientific brethren, is the commitment of each group to the pursuit of truth and to the assembling of demonstrable evidence. Skeat's often-expressed annoyance at the fanciful etymologies he encountered among supposedly authoritative writers is a result of this commitment. In *The Science of Etymology*, Skeat describes a typical bit of unwarranted creativity, a derivation of the word "foxglove," which, as Skeat explains, comes from the Anglo-Saxon for "fox's glove" and refers, with a genuine fillip of fancy, to the appearance of the blossoms of this plant, a member of the digitalis family. But the target of Skeat's ire has gone a bit further. Preferring fairies to foxes, he has explained the word as "folk's glove,"

> with reference to the "little folk" or fairies . . . I am told there are some who admire the name, because it is so "poetical." But this does not alter the fact that it is entirely false. . . . the business of the student of language is to ascertain what were the actual forms of names in olden times, and not to be wise above what is written by inventing names which our forefathers *ought* to have employed. The philologist is not concerned with what ought to have been said; his business is to pursue strictly historical methods. It would be strange indeed if we were to extend similar methods to history; as, for instance, by asserting that Anne Boleyn was never beheaded, because she ought not to have been. [12]

Just as the scientific principles of etymology should be respected, in Skeat's view, so should any related controversy be carried on simply as a search for truth. In collecting his contributions to *Notes and Queries*, that arena for more or less gracious disagreement, Skeat reflects upon the distance which some of his contemporaries had to travel in this regard:

> If a man has a good case, he can base it upon facts and quotations; and it is no answer to tell me, when I ask for proof, that it is ungentlemanly to dare to contradict. Moreover, it is very strange, as I have often argued, that it is only in the case of etymology that such tactics are resorted to. If the question were one of chemistry, botany, or any form of science, the appeal would lie to the facts; and we should be amazed if anyone who asserted that the chief constituents of water are oxygen and nitrogen were to take offense at contradiction. The whole matter lies in a nutshell; if etymology is to be scientific, the appeal lies to the facts; and the facts, in this case, are accurate quotations, with exact references, from all available authors. To attempt to etymologize without the help of quotations, is like learning geology without inspecting specimens; and we may well ask, what good can come of it?[13]

Latin Pronunciation and English Spelling

Another significant action in the battle for philological truth took place not in the field of English but in that of Latin, although the English scholars were involved to some extent. The grounds for the dispute were the shifting of English vowel sounds. These had over the centuries undergone some curious changes, while the alphabetical letters used to represent them had remained the same.

The Anglo-Saxon scholars of the nineteenth century, as they began to realize there was a discrepancy, set out to educate themselves, assisted by the newly discovered laws governing such changes. Skeat tells us that he himself once knew no better than to give the long vowel *i* the sound it has in the modern English *ride*, rather than the less frequent (in English) pronunciation of *i* in *machine*. Anglo-Saxon sounds were fairly quickly put to rights, as the small band of scholars in charge of them was a limber and innovative body; but then an analogous error suggested itself. The Anglo-Saxon manuscripts had been written in the Roman alphabet, that being the alphabet closest to hand, and the sounds represented by the symbols would then have been the same in Latin as in Anglo-Saxon. What followed was the suspicion that Latin, too, was being mispronounced.

The resulting controversy was long and emotional. Unlike Anglo-Saxon, Latin possessed a complex educational hierarchy in England and elsewhere; tens of thousands of children sat down to study Latin every day. Thousands of teachers taught it. The old traditions were highly respected, so that it did little good to explain that the original pronunciations represented an even older tradition. Furthermore, a certain resentment for the brash new philologists had begun to accumulate, and it is possible that their suggestions—or their unasked-for bossings about, as the Latinists saw it—might have fallen on stony ground no matter what they happened to be. The realignment took decades. In general, it was the newer institutions which were the first to change their Latin vowels, throwing in for good measure a few consonents which turned out to have been incorrectly represented in the alphabet. But in England's more venerable halls of learning, professors and students continued in the old ways, pronouncing Latin as their fathers and grandfathers had done, and staunchly quoted Caesar's summary of his activities abroad as "venny, viddy, vicky."

Having supported the past with regard to the pronouncing of Latin, Skeat perhaps surprisingly turned to the future with regard to the spelling of English. In collusion once again with Furnivall, he founded the Simplifed Spelling Society at the turn of the century and as first president delivered an address in Winchester, on the occasion of the millenary celebration of the reign of King Alfred. Skeat may have startled his colleagues by his breezy approach: "In the interests of etymology we ought to spell as we pronounce. To spell words as they *used* to be pronounced is not etymological, but antiquarian."

Several years later, in a series of pamphlets brought out by the Simplified Spelling Society, Skeat and his associates took a logical next step; having written the first number in conventional spelling, they brought out the second in a simplified form, thus practicing what they preached. The passage quoted above from Skeat's speech at Winchester, reprinted on the inside front cover as part of the Society's manifesto, came out as follows:

In dhe interests ov etimolojy we aut to spel as we pronouns.
To spel wurdz as dhae *uest* to be pronounst iz not etimolo-
jikal, but antikwaeryan.[14]

That these lines look as odd to the present-day reader as they did to
the original ones is of course an indication of the large scale of the task
which Skeat and his Society had set themselves, and an indication also
that neither they nor any of the several bodies then working toward the
same goal had any lasting or extensive effect on English spelling, at
least as far as the twentieth century has been concerned. The picture
may change any day.

The Elrington and Bosworth Chair of Anglo-Saxon

We left Skeat as a tutor of mathematics, quietly inserting English language and literature into the intellectual atmosphere of Cambridge.
His efforts were to be officially recognized in the late 1870s. For the
background, we need to look at Oxford, where the study of Anglo-
Saxon had been officially under way since the establishment of the
Rawlinson Chair in 1795. Here the prevailing sentiment was that while
the English language in its early forms was an acceptable academic
discipline, English literature was not. Cambridge was to become more
inclusive. In any case, the holder of the Rawlinson Chair in 1868,
Joseph Bosworth, felt so strongly that his subject should be encouraged
at the sister University that he gave a sum of money to establish a chair
in it. (The "Elrington" of the title honored the memory of Bosworth's
wife, who had helped him in the compilation of his Anglo-Saxon
dictionaries.) Bosworth's chair was not quite the first effort in this line
at Cambridge. In the early seventeenth century, before the English
Civil War, a lectureship in Anglo-Saxon had been set up by the historian Henry Spelman; but the foundation had not survived.

Events moved slowly even after Bosworth's gift. The sum was not
sufficient to provide a dignified stipend, so an arrangement was agreed
upon whereby it would be left to accumulate until the interest reached
£500 annually, at which time an occupant of the chair would be chosen. This moment arrived in 1878. Bosworth had died two years previously, quite unfortunately, as he would have been interested in the
outcome and, from the evidence of a letter Skeat included in his port-

folio of testimonials, would have been happy to see the chair go to Skeat. This letter, written in 1871, thanks the officials of the Cambridge University Press for having sent him a copy of Skeat's edition of *The Gospel of St. Mark*, a parallel text arrangement of eight Anglo-Saxon manuscripts, and incidentally provides us with another glimpse of scholarly life before the days of photocopiers and word processors:

> [I]nstead of having the trouble of referring to the manuscripts or the various books in which some of them are printed, I find [in Skeat's edition], at once, all I want to quote in my large Anglo Saxon dictionary, preparing for the Clarendon Press, in which I and my amanuenses are employed at least seven hours a day.[15]

Bosworth goes on to hope that similar editions of Luke and John will appear—"I believe it would be difficult to find so good an editor as Mr. Skeat"—and Skeat accordingly undertook the work, bringing it close to completion by the time of his application for the Elrington and Bosworth chair. "The Anglo-Saxon portion is easy enough," he then observed of the project, "but the Old Northumbrian requires the minutest care."[16]

Skeat's wholehearted and energetic pursuit of the Elrington and Bosworth Chair seems at first glance rather disconcerting, out of character somehow for a mild-mannered philologist. However, things were often done this way. A professorial appointment at either of the two traditional universities was a major event in the eye of the public, leading members of which tended to be alumni, and to appear diffident about one's candidacy might have been read as a sign of disrespect. Skeat's collection of forty-eight testimonial letters, printed by the Cambridge University Press as a fifty-six page book, raised no eyebrows at all.

This document, containing as Skeat explains letters from "nearly every Professor, teacher and editor of English whose opinion can be supposed to have much weight," provides something of a cross-section of the academic progress of the new subject by the year 1878. From the German universities, where philological studies had first gained momentum at the beginning of the century, came testimonials from Bernhard Ten Brink at Strassburg and Julius Zupitza at Berlin; from England's growing industrial cities, whose universities had been founded only within the past decade or so, fully fledged Professors of

English cheered Cambridge's commendable if belated effort to catch up. The United States, Ireland, and the colonies were not left out. Not all the responses came from universities; the study of English had strong proponents in the world of letters generally, and encouragement arrived from the desks of authors, librarians, editors.

The content and tone of these recommendations provide little by way of surprise. The writers declared themselves unanimously pro-Skeat. Some variety does ensue as the writers face the task of making what must have struck them as a redundantly obvious statement. James A. H. Murray, editor in chief of the *Oxford English Dictionary*, begins point-blank: "No more superfluous task could be imposed upon any English scholar than that of bearing his testimony to the fitness of the Rev. W. W. Skeat to fill the Anglo-Saxon chair at Cambridge." Other respondents sought to prod Cambridge into an awareness of the global nature of her academic choices: "The carefulness and thoroughness of Mr. Skeat's work are acknowledged by every English scholar on the Continent, in our Colonies, America, and Great Britain," says Furnivall, implying perhaps that the University would be subject to international ridicule should she fail to take up this opportunity. Francis Child, writing from Harvard, shows a hint of his characteristic impatience at England's slow progress in using her human as well as her textual resources: "The state of Anglo-Saxon learning at present in England is such as to make recruits of Mr. Skeat's activity and scholarship particularly desirable."[17]

A few respondents admitted to knowing Skeat only through his works rather than personally—among them George Webbe Dasent, author of *Popular Tales from the Norse*, and David Masson in Edinburgh—while others stated that their own expertise lay elsewhere than in Anglo-Saxon. Edward Dowden, then occupying the first English chair (established in 1867) at Trinity College, Dublin, explains that Skeat's speciality is a bit early for him but adds, apparently from a familiar professorial assumption that his or her own preference lies at the true heart of the matter, "It is an advantage, I think, that his interest in our literature runs on to Elizabethan and to recent times." Henry Morley, on the other hand, feels at home in Anglo-Saxon; writing from University College, where endowed chairs were not a standard part of the academic furniture and where attracting fee-paying students was a necessary concern of any discipline, he reassures the Cambridge authorities that this particular ancient language is a viable concern—at least, he cannot help implying, where it is properly taught: "Since 1859—for the last eighteen or nineteen years—first in the evening classes at King's College and then here, I have taught Anglo-Saxon in London, and believe that I am the only teacher who for so long a time has in no session failed to form a class."[18]

A specific and quite timely angle, since women's education had become a lively concern at Cambridge with the founding of Girton College in 1869 and Newnham College in 1871, appears in the letter of Henry Sidgwick, secretary to the Association for the Promotion of the Higher Education of Women in Cambridge:

> I have much pleasure in bearing testimony to the ungrudging manner in which you have devoted time and trouble to the Higher Education of Women, since the first institution of the Lectures for Women in Cambridge. You have lectured every year since 1870—and, I am glad to say, to increased numbers in later years—on Chaucer, Spenser, Shakespeare, and other English writers. For the last three years you have also given lectures on Anglo-Saxon; to classes small, indeed, but composed of serious students.[19]

And finally, taking its rightful place among the letters of Skeat's colleagues, appears that most authoritative of testimonials, the former student doing well. T. N. Toller, identifying himself as "Lecturer on the English Language at the Owens College, Manchester," writes:

> I am glad that at last there is to be a Professor of Anglo-Saxon, and I hope most sincerely that you may be the first to occupy the new chair. And indeed, I have good reason to wish you success in your candidature; for ever since I began to read Anglo-Saxon with you, six years ago, I have found you most ready with your assistance in all matters connected with English.
>
> I hope now that you are about to find a good number of students to whom, as Professor, you will have an opportunity of doing those good offices which you did to me, when there was no recognized teacher of the subject.[20]

It may come as something of an anticlimax to learn that Skeat did after all get the job.

The Medieval and Modern Languages Tripos

Among the first of Skeat's accomplishments upon his being named to the Bosworth and Elrington chair was the establishment in 1878 of an honors examination—a "Tripos" in Cambridge terminology—designed to be challenging enough to attract good students and thus to establish the discipline of modern languages and literature as the worthwhile subject which Skeat and his colleagues naturally believed it to be. Thus for the first time an undergraduate might earn an honors degree for his knowledge of his native language and its literary treasures. In the 1878 version of the examination, English could be presented only in combination with either French or German; but in 1890 the examination was further modified, until the rather complicated options allowed a student to elect English as a specialty unto itself.[21] The work was based solidly on the earlier forms of the language.

The word *tripos*, Cambridge slang for the honors examination, derived neither from a three-part division (which might accidentally be the case) nor from the fact that a student sat for it in his or her third year (which usually was the case in the nineteenth century, as it happened), but ultimately from the three-legged stool the examiner had sat upon, back in the Middle Ages, while questioning the candidate. Traditions at Cambridge can have long roots. The word is peculiar to Cambridge; at Oxford and elsewhere, exams are exams.

A candidate for the Medieval and Modern Language Tripos in 1890—the first year in which a Cambridge undergraduate might, if he wished, specialize in English—would make a choice of two of the following six options:

(A) English language and literature from the Middle English period to the present.

(B) English language and literature from the Anglo-Saxon to the Middle English period; Anglo-French or Icelandic; Gothic.

(C) French language and literature from 1500 to the present.

(D) French language and literature before 1500; Provençal, or Spanish or Portuguese writings earlier than 1350; Romance phonology, morphology, and syntax.

(E) German language and literature from 1500 to the present.

(F) Old and Middle High German; Gothic; German grammar and principles of Teutonic philology.[22]

A candidate electing to do all his work in English, sections (A) and (B) above, would then face as his examination, spread over a two-week period, a total of twelve three-hour papers. (The medieval custom of oral examinations had changed over the centuries. Victorian candidates used up a great deal of ink.) Each of these papers dealt with a specific question in the following areas:

[from Section (A)]

(1) Passages from specified and unspecified works of Shakespeare for explanation and discussion; with questions and subjects for essays on language, meter and literary history.

(2) Passages from specified and unspecified English authors not earlier than 1500, exclusive of Shakespeare, for explanation and discussion; with questions on language and literary history.

(3) (a) Passages from specified and unspecified English authors not earlier than 1500, exclusive of Shakespeare.
    (b) Passages from selected English prose and verse writings between 1200 and 1500, exclusive of Chaucer.

(4) Passages from selected English prose and verse writings between 1200 and 1500, exclusive of Chaucer.

(5) Passages from specified and unspecified works of Chaucer.

(6) Passages from selected prose and verse writings in the Wessex dialect of Old English.

[from Section (B)]

(1) Passages from English prose and verse writings between 1100 and 1400.

(2) Passages from prose and verse writings in Old English earlier than 1100 for translation and explanation.

(3) Passages from selected writings in Old English for translation and explanation.

(4) (a) Passages from selected writings in Anglo-French for translation and explanation.
    (b) Passages from selected writings in Icelandic.

(5) Passages from Wulfila for translation and explanation; with questions on the Gothic language.

(6) Questions on historical English grammar (including phonology, morphology and syntax), and on the principles of Teutonic philology with special reference to the languages included in this section.[23]

The (a) and (b) subsections listed here represent either/or options, while the rather disconcerting repetition built into the choices serves to insure that the candidate prepare some areas in more depth. The candidate would of course expect to write two different essays should he choose both question (2) and question (3a) in Section A, for example, even though the area covered is the same. The transcription given here is slightly simplified, as most items go on to specify "questions and subjects for essays on language, meter, and literary history."

While honors candidates worked toward their sufficiently grisly set of final hurdles, the majority of undergraduates, candidates for the "ordinary B.A. degree" as the University *Calendar* puts it, found English language and literature a necessary part of their studies as well. The ordinary B.A. of the 1890s required both a "general" examination in a large number of subjects and a "special" examination on some chosen field. (This combination, a panorama of many subjects with a close-up view of one in particular, is similar in its basic plan to many liberal arts degrees in the twentieth century.) These two examinations for the "ordinary B.A." were not required of honors candidates, who had their own worries at this point; but honors candidates along with their "ordinary B.A." colleagues had passed a set of so-called "previous" examinations, a sort of warm-up, the year before and thus could be certified as having acquired some knowledge in breadth.

Among the many challenges in the "general examination" was the chance to write a voluntary essay on "some play of Shakespeare or some portion of the works of Milton," the examiners having been cautioned in the meantime to choose well-known subjects, so that "everyone who is examined may be reasonably expected to shew a competent knowledge of them." The rising water table of undergraduate awareness of English literature is perhaps demonstrated here. This voluntary essay was not required, in that one could get a degree without it, but, says the *Calendar* sternly, "the results shall be taken into account in assigning the places in the Class-Lists."[24]

For the second part of his examination, the special subject, the "ordinary B.A." candidate might choose from the following list, an interesting one as it allows a quick look at the branches of knowledge which Cambridge considered worthwhile in the 1890s: Theology, Logic, Political Economy, Law, History, Chemistry, Physics, Geology, Botany, Zoology, Physiology, Mechanism and Applied Science, Music, Modern Languages, Mathematics, Classics. The reader can probably think of gaps in this array, but certainly Cambridge at the end of the century was making an effort to augment the curriculum of theology, classics, and mathematics to which she had felt herself restricted by tradition only a few decades earlier, when Skeat was an undergraduate.

A studen choosing "modern languages'" as his special subject then faced a further choice, as he might be examined in either English or French, or English and German. Either option called for some work in early forms of the language, with an opportunity to go even farther back in time; voluntary papers, on the same principle as those mentioned above, might be written on elementary Anglo-Saxon or Middle High German, with, adds the *Calendar* reassuringly of the latter, "easy questions on historical Grammar."

Oxford Repels English Literature

Thanks perhaps to Skeat's matter-of-fact insistence that language and literature might be studied together, and also perhaps to Skeat's highly visible and (for the uninitiated) rather terrifying emphasis on the philological aspects of his discipline, Cambridge did not find itself at daggers drawn over the question of admitting English literature to the curriculum. It was firmly bound in with linguistic studies, but it was there. Oxford, however, proved to be another kettle of fish. With the establishment of the Merton Professorship of English Language and Literature in 1880, and the subsequent controversy over who was to fill the chair and what exactly was to be taught from it, the discipline of English as it applied to higher education became a matter of public concern.

The controversy was quite an energetic one. Letters filled the columns of the *Times*, essays and counteressays appeared in the quarterlies. (The *Contemporary Review*, the *Pall Mall Gazette*, and the *Edinburgh Review* were particularly hospitable to these exchanges.)

Among the foremost of the antiliterature faction was E. A. Freeman, Oxford's Professor of Modern History, who despite the first impression one might gain from his title stood firmly for a traditional curriculum. The *Times* in May of 1887 (seven years after the establishment of the disputed and as yet unfilled chair—things moved slowly) quoted Freeman's questioning of "what was meant by distinguishing literature from language, if by literature was intended the study of great books, and not mere chatter about Shelley"; immediately "chatter about Shelley" became a rallying cry for opponents of the innovation.[25] John Earle, at that time occupant of the Rawlinson Chair of Anglo-Saxon, was also much against the introduction of English literature as a degree subject.

Freeman, Earle, and their supporters found much to be dubious about. What sort of examination questions could be asked? (Skeat, though debate of this sort was not his element, had earlier tried to be of use in this particular perplexity, publishing in 1873 a small book, *Questions for Examination in English Literature*, containing sample questions he had himself used and found effective. This compilation did not seem to have been noticed at Oxford.) Could one, the professors pondered, examine in taste? The shadow of belles lettres, in which literature might appear as a kind of accessory to the formation of aesthetic judgments, seemed to hang over the landscape. If candidates were to be asked to go beyond mere facts and dates, to support critical opinions, might they not simply memorize an opinion they had found somewhere else? The whole endeavor, it was feared, would be dilettantish; no reliable standards seemed to exist; English literature was simply too nebulous. Undergraduates might be drawn to it because it looked easy. These forebodings in fact represent quite valid causes for concern, even though the obstacles have since proved not to be insurmountable. Oxford hesitated. The best solution, many felt, would be simply to appoint another philologist to the Merton professorship and let the University continue in the direction in which it felt comfortable.

Against this consensus there arose a champion of great determination. John Churton Collins was a University Extension lecturer in English literature, a preparer of candidates for the Civil Service examinations (in which English literature had been one of the set subjects for some decades now), an editor of English literature busily preparing for the press sets of the works of Dryden, Pope, Tennyson, and many others. Collins was in fact somewhat similar to Henry Morley, lacking the latter's enthusiasm for the early phases of the English language and lacking as well Morley's tact, good humor, and ability to adapt to circumstances.

Collins had a specific idea of how English literature should be taught—not, he said, in an isolated philological context but in relation to the classical masterpieces which had influenced its development.[26] Milton should be read in connection with Virgil, not with *Beowulf*. Considering Oxford's positive attitude toward classical literature, one might be surprised that Collins's attitude was not welcomed, and more surprised perhaps in view of the fact that Collins was an Oxford man, having developed his love for the classics at Balliol College.

But Oxford did not welcome her native son. Collins put himself forward as a candidate for the Merton Professorship, not an unusual move, as we have seen; but Collins's manner of proceeding was an upsetting one. He campaigned not only for himself but for his dream, the setting up of an honors school of English in every British university. Collins expounded the details of this project in the quarterly reviews. To gather support, he sent out a questionnaire, phrased in such a way as to make negative or even hedged replies look like a vote against literature, to influential people, some of whom (e.g., the politician John Bright) had little to do with either literature or higher education; he then published the replies. His victims protested, also in print. Collins's single-minded zeal gave him tunnel vision to a remarkable degree. At one point, to prove that English literature is based upon that of ancient Greece and Rome, Collins published an analysis of Tennyson's poetry tracing influences to their sources so minutely that Tennyson appeared merely to have put together a series of pastiches; Collins was perplexed when this effort earned him the enmity of the Laureate, with whom he had considered himself on terms of comfortable acquaintanceship.

Not surprisingly, Collins's denunciation of philology was severe. Summing up his views several years later, he writes:

> As an instrument of culture it [philology] ranks—it surely ranks—very low indeed. It certainly contributes nothing to the cultivation of the taste. It as certainly contributes nothing to the education of the emotions. The mind it neither en- larges, stimulates, nor refines. On the contrary, it too often induces or confirms that peculiar woodenness and opacity,

and intellectual vision, which has in all ages been the characteristic of mere philologists. [27]

It is possible that, had the cause of English literature only been advocated by someone else, Oxford might have looked on it with more favor. It may be comforting to note that some years later Collins finally did become a Professor of English at the University of Birmingham. Here he settled down, worked amicably with his colleagues, and won praise from his students for his knowledge, his patience, and his concern for their progress. One might say that a classful of students will bring out the best in anybody. But Collins was not a bad person, only stubborn and strangely naive. Meanwhile at Oxford, the Merton Professorship went to A. S. Napier, a philologist who, according to A. C. Partridge, "lectured on no author later than Chaucer." [28]

It was not until almost twenty years later, in 1904, that Oxford had another chance to revise the English curriculum, and she then did so quite decisively. English literature and language were divided into separate chairs, and the occupant of the literature chair, Walter Raleigh (at one time a student of Henry Morley's), then went on to establish Oxford's honors school of English. Oxford was then further along the road to today's notions of the disciplinary boundaries than Cambridge, as the latter was not to separate literature and philology until 1917.

The separation of language and literature did not mean at either university that *Beowulf* or Chaucer in all their linguistic complexity was dropped from the canon. Students of literature still learned Anglo-Saxon and Middle English, but they might concentrate on those dialects which happened to contain works of literary value, and they no longer needed to delve into Icelandic or Old Norse for the sake of verbal cognates.

Cambridge Rounds the Century

E. M. W. Tillyard, whose *The Muse Unchained: An Intimate Account of the Revolution in English Studies at Cambridge* continues the fortunes of the new discipline into the twentieth century, sees Skeat and his contemporaries more or less as patriarchs from a former age:

Sentimentally I think of Skeat along with David Masson as heroic figures in Victorian scholarship. Skeat, the Anglican mathematician, was drier and more precise; Masson, the Non-conformist, could be sentimental and sanctimonious; but they were alike in the sense they give of space, leisure, of there being "world enough and time." They really set their minds on what they were doing, and were quite certain it was worth while. That others might not think so either never occurred to them, or, if it did, failed to disturb them. Masson's lavishness in his *Life of Milton* is vast; to make sure, he throws in heaps of information that has [sic] no visible bearing on his subject. Skeat in elaborating a note on Chaucer does not hesitate to indulge the heat of his own interest rather than his reader's more modest wishes. They both remind me of those great Victorian kitchen ranges which in spite of the formidable waste of fuel and heat did end by warming the bath-water and by loading the table with something which however heavy was certainly food. [29]

Naturally, Skeat would have been unlikely to view his career in quite this way, since one generation's notion of an efficient way to complete a scholarly project might differ considerably from that of the next. Different needs are perceived. To Skeat, he himself played the roler of an explorer, writing with an explorer's zeal; a tangential addition to a philological note seems less tangential if it has about it the burnish of the new.

Since Skeat's public image did not include an exhausting round of lectures, either to the general public or to undergraduates, his retirement was a gradual one, and the basic ingredients of his life stayed the same. He prepared a revised and enlarged edition of his *Etymological Dictionary* (which first appeared in 1879) for publication in 1910, two years before his death. He continued to frequent the libraries of Cambridge and to walk the streets and cloisters of the town, which (with the exception of his years as a curate) he had made his home for almost sixty years. Skeat and his growing family had lived in several parts of Cambridge, the shifting addresses being faithfully recorded in the membership lists of the Early English Text Society.

Skeat was also at home in Oxford, where his philological associates had become faithful friends. K. M. Elisabeth Murray, in her *Caught in the Web of Words*, describes a jaunt which Skeat and James Murray took on the latter's tandem tricycle in the 1880s; tricycles—quite large ones—were the latest thing, and the two up-to-date gentlemen, each turned fifty-years-old or almost, wheeled through the streets in the dignity of their scholarly white beards.[30]

The Tripos which Skeat designed in 1890 (officially instituted in 1891) sums up Skeat's vision of English studies as a discipline. This moment in time has proved, as we have observed, a transitory one. The discipline was poised to proliferate. Freeing English literature from the yoke of philology (as the situation was perceived by the advocates of literature—advocates whose position rather baffled Skeat) was the next item on the agenda. Although this development was a natural one, appearing in English departments wherever in the world they had been set up, events at Cambridge were considered influential and are well documented; Tillyard's book, quoted above, deals with them and so does Stephen Potter's earlier *The Muse in Chains: A Study in Education* (1937).

Skeat had observed the growth of English studies at Cambridge and elsewhere with pleasure during the last half of his lifetime. He was instrumental in the appointment of Israel Gollancz, one of his former students, as the University's first Lecturer in English Literature in 1896. (Gollancz later continued his distinguished career at University College.) Although Skeat naturally did not know who his own successor would be, the successful candidate for the Elrington and Bosworth Chair, H. M. Chadwick, brought English studies at Cambridge to another milestone; with Arthur Quiller-Couch, holder of the newly-endowed (1910) King Edward VII Chair of English, Chadwick was a major founder of the English School at Cambridge in 1917. The Tripos put into effect at this time separated language and literature more definitely than the version of the 1890s had done, although yet another step in this direction was taken in 1926.

All this seeming antiphilological activity had no negative effect on the philologists themselves, who simply kept on studying their field and solving the problems they discovered. There are still professors and students dealing with the older forms of Icelandic, at Cambridge and elsewhere. What happened was that the image of the English student changed from that of a linguist to that of a literary critic, both at least in embryo; consequently, the label itself seemed to have become more specific. It is perhaps ironic that some of Skeat's work—his dictionaries, his editions, his philological notes—should have struck academic heirs as old-fashioned, relics of a past era. Philological studies did more than impress onlookers with the complexity of the new discipline; they provided a bedrock without which studies of literature might well have been somewhat shaky, and they have continued to feed back into the mainstream of English studies (however varyingly this mainstream happens to be labelled) valuable contributions in the way of facts, theories, insights. After all, the relationship between English philology and English literature did not come to an end just because a student could get a degree in one without the other. Skeat and his colleagues, busy mapping and plotting the unknown land into which they had sallied forth, thus served a more vital function than the beneficiaries of their labors often recognize. Certainly Skeat, for all his modesty, might have assured himself that in his life and work he had achieved his "object as regards this present world," that of rendering some help to his fellow creatures.

Notes

Chapter 1

1. A. C. Partridge, *Landmarks in the History of English Scholarship 1500–1970* (Capetown, South Africa: Nasou Limited, 1972), p. 5.

2. Hugh Hale Bellot, "The Admission of Women," in *University College, London, 1826–1926* (London: University of London Press, 1929), pp. 367–73.

3. "English literature has always been regarded, for good or evil, as a subject peculiarly fitted for the education of women, and as that movement [women's education] gathered force in the second half of the century, so English studies were carried with it to the very doors of the ancient universities." David J. Palmer, *The Rise of English Studies: An Account of the Study of English Language and Literature from Its Origins to the Making of the Oxford English School* (Oxford: Oxford University Press, 1965), p. 38.

4. "It was the opening up of India, and the discovery of Sanskrit by European, and especially English, scholars at the end of the eighteenth century which brought about a new view." Raymond Wilson Chambers, *Man's Unconquerable Mind: Studies of English Writers from Bede to A. E. Housman and W. P. Kerr* (London: Jonathan Cape, 1952), p. 344. Chambers's eleventh chapter, "Philologists at University College" (delivered as a centenary address in 1927), contains a brisk and informative survey of these philological events.

5. The present reader's old textbooks may well supply this information and much else besides; but the bare bones of linguistic theories have become easily accessible to the public. This list of consonants appears under "Grimm's Law" in the *American Heritage Dictionary*, 2d college ed. (1982).

6. The *Cambridge History of American Literature*, vol. 4 (New York: Putnam, 1921), pp. 451–68, gives a detailed account of the German influence upon scholarship in nineteenth-century America, covering, of course, other disciplines besides English. Especially prominent were George Ticknor of Harvard, who studied Greek at Göttingen, and Basil Lanneau Gildersleeve, first of the University of Virginia and later (for most of his career) of Johns Hopkins, who studied Greek and Latin at Berlin, Bonn, and Göttingen.

7. Partridge, *Landmarks*, pp. 5–7.

8. A brief and quite accessible description of the groundbreaking labors of the *Oxford English Dictionary* can be found in the "Historical Introduction" to the first volume of that work, pp. vii–xxvi. More details, and some useful

explanations of the *Dictionary*'s context in Victorian life generally, appear in *Caught in the Web of Words: James A. H. Murray and the Oxford Dictionary* (New Haven: Yale University Press, 1977), by the editor's granddaughter, K. M. Elisabeth Murray.

9. See Walter Scott Achtert, "Editing Societies," in "A History of English Studies to 1883 Based on the Research of William Riley Parker," (Ph.D. diss., New York University, 1972), pp. 182–87.

10. The E.E.T.S. continues to flourish in the 1980s, with a membership of around 1,250 and headquarters in Oxford. Some of the earlier issues are now being reedited. A dark period occurred in 1914–18 when, as the 1931 volume of the Society's *Annual Report* notes, "the war with its widespread interruption of communications almost reduced the Society to bankruptcy"; but rescue came from the Carnegie Trustees of America in 1918.

11. They appear in the 1866–67 volume of the University College, London, annual *Calendar*, where examination questions in most disciplines are itemized. Henry Morley was at that time Professor of English.

12. For understandable reasons, reprints of the E.E.T.S. editions omit much of the original chit-chat from editors to subscribers, and it is only in surviving copies from these early days (copies which have often been read to a state of dilapidation) that one comes across such announcements. This one appeared in several issues in the 1870s. The saints' lives duly followed, and it would seem that the subscribers bit the bullet and bought them.

13. William Riley Parker, in "The MLA, 1883–1953," *PMLA* 68 (September 1953), part 2, pp. 3–39, gives a careful account of the association's early years. While much of his material can be found on the shelves of libraries whose files of *PMLA* go back to the founding of the journal in 1885, Parker adds color and background, giving contemporary newspapers' reports of the meetings and describing the careers of the participants.

14. Thomas W. Hart, Professor of Rhetoric and the English Language at the College of New Jersey, Princeton, made this plea, preserved in the 1884 volume of the association's *Proceedings* (superseded by *PMLA*).

15. Parker, "The MLA," p. 12.

16. Ibid., p. 22.

17. Palmer, in *The Rise of English Studies*, pp. 29–40, describes a number of examples.

18. A revealing variety of firsthand accounts by former students can be found in the Rev. John Llewelyn Davies, ed., *The Working Men's College 1854–1904: Records of Its History and Work for Fifty Years* (London: Macmillan, 1904).

19. John H. Fisher, "Nationalism and the Study of Literature," *American Scholar* 49 (Winter 1979–80), p. 105.

20. Ibid., p. 107.

21. See "Baconian theory" in *The Reader's Encyclopedia of Shakespeare*, ed. O. J. Campbell and E. G. Quinn (New York: Crowell, 1966).

22. Dewey Ganzel, *Fortune and Men's Eyes: The Career of John Payne Collier* (Oxford: Oxford University Press, 1982). Ganzel's minute investigation

gives us a view of the high level of public interest in literary questions of the day. This one, admittedly, was more sensational than most; but the publications Ganzel cites—the *Athenaum, Notes and Queries, Fraser's Magazine*, and of course *The Times*—often served as forums for scholarly controversy.

23. Achtert, "A History of English Studies to 1883," pp. 77–78.

24. *Encyclopaedia Britannica*, 11th ed. (1911).

Chapter 2

1. Hugh Hale Bellot's exhaustive *University College, London, 1826–1916* is my main authority for nineteenth-century details about the College.

2. King's College was located (and still is) on the Strand, opposite St. Mary le Strand Church; it was close enough geographically to Bloomsbury to enjoy a rivalry with University College in what we might call informal student recreations. Some are described in David Taylor's *The Godless Students of Gower Street* (London: University College Union, 1968).

3. Stephen Potter quotes at length from Dale's speeches and writings in *The Muse in Chains: A Study in Education* (London: Jonathan Cape, 1937), pp. 143–45.

4. Morley is the beneficiary of a typical Victorian "family" biography, written shortly after his death by his admiring son-in-law, Henry Shaen Solly. *The Life of Henry Morley, LL.D.* (London: Edward Arnold, 1898) quotes extensively from Morley's letters and publications, and includes as well memorials written at Solly's request by friends, family members, and former students. Most of the details given here of Morley's life come from this source; others are from a collection of Morley's personal writings, *Early Papers and Some Memories* (London: G. Routledge and Sons, 1891).

5. Reprinted from *Household Words*, in Morley, *Early Papers and Some Memories*.

6. Solly, *Life of Henry Morley*, p. 233.

7. Ibid.

8. René Wellek's *The Rise of English Literary History* (Chapel Hill: University of North Carolina Press, 1941) traces the development of this art through the eighteenth century, focusing on Thomas Warton, whose *History of English Poetry* (1774–1781) Wellek sees as the first major accomplishment in this line. "Literary history as a distinct discipline," Wellek points out, "arose only when biography and criticism coalesced and when, under the influence of political historiography, the narrative form began to be used," p. 1.

9. Potter accuses the University of London, in particular, of a "tendency to reduce literature to its verifiable constituents," *The Muse in Chains*, p. 155.

10. This list comes from the University College *Calendar* for 1865–66 and shows few major changes through the next three decades.

11. From the University College *Calendar*, 1889–90. Since University of London examinations were taken by candidates from all the constituent colleges, this annual list would appear in each of the respective calendars and also in official publications of the University of London. Thus the subjects set by

the examiners would have a very definite impact on the literature studied in a large number of classrooms.

12. University College *Calendar*, 1889–90.

13. University College *Calendar*, 1888–89. Today's students, as they deliberate on whether or not to enroll in a course, might envy their nineteenth-century counterparts' access to the previous year's exam questions printed up more or less as part of the course description.

14. Solly, *Life of Henry Morley*, p. 261.

15. University College *Calendar*, 1888–89.

16. Solly, *Life of Henry Morley*, pp. 259–60.

17. Ibid., pp. 284–85.

18. Morley, *A First Sketch of English Literature* (London: Cassell and Co., 1873), pp. 87–88.

19. Solly, *Life of Henry Morley*, pp. 356–57.

20. Palmer, *The Rise of English Studies*, p. 50.

Chapter 3

1. George L. Kittredge, "Francis James Child," in Child's *The English and Scottish Popular Ballads* 1 (1882), xxiii. This essay appears in editionss printed after 1896. Dixwell's financial aid to Child is occasionally mentioned by other writers (who may have been influenced by Kittredge's essay), but I have not found a statement by Child, or any details as to the amount.

2. James Donald Reppert, *F. J. Child and the Ballad* (Ph.D. diss., Harvard University, 1953), p. 2.

3. *Report of the President*, Harvard College, 1845–46. Child was a senior in that year.

4. Kermit Vanderbilt, *Charles Eliot Norton: Apostle of Culture in a Democracy* (Cambridge, Mass.: Harvard University Press, 1959), p. 26.

5. Francis James Child, ed., *Four Old Plays* (Cambridge, Mass.: George Nichols, 1848), p. xvii.

6. Matthew Arnold, *Higher Schools and Universities in Germany* (London: Macmillan, 1868. 2d ed., 1882), pp. 143–44.

7. Kittredge, "Francis James Child," p. xxv.

8. As the reader has probably concluded, college catalogues of the nineteenth century usually contained a great deal more news than is the case today, and these titles come from this source. However, the Harvard archives preserve a number of the actual essays, beautifully written out on good paper, as stipulated by the rules for the Bowdoin prize.

9. Harvard College *Catalogue*, 1853–54.

10. Ibid.

11. Ibid.

12. Harvard College *Catalogue*, 1863–64.

13. *Boston Evening Transcript*, September 12, 1896. From Kittredge's scrapbook of press cuttings in the Harvard University Archives.

14. Francis Gummere, *The Nation*, June 16, 1898. A review of the final

volume of *The English and Scottish Popular Ballads*, prepared by Kittredge after Child's death.

15. Francis Gummere, "A Day with Professor Child," *Atlantic Monthly* 103 (March 1909), p. 423.

16. Harvard College *Catalogue*. 1891–92.

17. Robert Grant, "Harvard College in the Seventies," *Scribner's Magazine* 21 (May 1897), p. 560.

18. Harvard College *Catalogue*, 1874–75.

19. Sigurd Bernhard Hustvedt, *Ballad Books and Ballad Men* (Cambridge, Mass.: Harvard University Press, 1930), p. 223.

20. *The English and Scottish Popular Ballads*, vol. 5, p. 59; commentary on ballad 272, "The Suffolk Miracle."

21. A more accessible sample of this type of correspondence, demonstrating Child's thoroughness and that of his helpers, appears in "The Gruntvig-Child Correspondence," Appendix A (pp. 241–300) of Hustvedt's *Ballad Books and Ballad Men*. The letters cover the period from 1872 to 1883. In 1883 Svendt Gruntvig died, having become world famous as a collector and editor of Danish ballads. Both sides of the correspondence were written in English.

22. Reppert, F. J. *Child and the Ballad*, p. 31.

23. Kittredge appears to have begun this collection on the occasion of Child's death, as most of the contents are obituary notices and brief memoirs.

24. Owned and run by Mr. and Mrs. Vangel L. Misho, "for lean-pocketed travellers," according to the advertisement in the Boston telephone directory's yellow pages. The present writer qualified on this score and could not resist moving in.

Chapter 4

1. *Dictionary of National Biography*, Supplement 1901–1911, pp. 583–85.

2. A detailed and perhaps suprisingly clear description of these events can be found in the *Encyclopedia Britannica*, 11th ed. (1911), in the article "Scotland, Church of."

3. Flora Masson, "David Masson," *University of Edinburgh Journal* 2 (1929–30), p. 22.

4. Richard D. Altick, *The English Common Reader: A Social History of the Mass Reading Public, 1800–1900* (Chicago: University of Chicago Press, 1957), pp. 81–85. Throughout this very useful book, Altick describes the rise in total population and the enlargement, within that population, of the social classes to whom the education, money, and spare time necessary for reading became increasingly accessible.

5. David Masson, *The British Museum: Historical and Descriptive* (Edinburgh: R. and W. Chambers, 1858), pp. 231–32.

6. Ibid., p. 232.

7. P. R. Harris, *The Reading Room* (London: The British Library, 1979), p. 22. A brief but informative pamphlet.

8. Bellot, *University College, London, 1826–1926*, pp. 46–47. "Half the professors," Bellot points out, "knew at first hand something of the educational systems of countries other than their own," p. 47.

9. See the *Wellesley Index to Victorian Periodicals 1824–1900*.

10. Potter, *The Muse in Chains*, p. 110. Potter gives a detailed description of the teaching of rhetoric, especially in Scotland, pp. 90–126.

11. Quoted in Palmer, *The Rise of English Studies*, p. 176.

12. Twenty-two years' worth of students' names are inscribed in Masson's hand in his enrollment book, a single volume covering 1866 through 1888, preserved in the University of Edinburgh's archives. The book does not record students' grades but does indicate that they all paid their fee for the course, three pounds three shillings throughout the period. On the back endpapers Masson listed his enrollment figures (171 in 1866, 194 in 1867, 175 in 1868, and so on), to a total of 4,579. As Masson did not retire until 1895, the next enrollment book would presumably have listed approximately 1,400 students.

13. From the 1866–67 University of Edinburgh *Calendar*, but repeated throughout Masson's career.

14. Ibid.; also repeated.

15. James Barrie, *An Edinburgh Eleven: Pencil Portraits of College Life* (London: Hodder and Stoughton, 1891), pp. 84–85.

16. David Rorie, "The Weighty Eighties," *University of Edinburgh Journal* 6 (1933–34), p. 12.

17. Ibid., p. 13.

18. Notebook of George Lumsden, who took Masson's course in 1881–82. First of two manuscript volumes; composition assignments listed on a back page.

19. Lumsden, vol. 1, lecture 16.

20. Notebook of Andrew David Sloane, one of Masson's students in 1882–83. First of three manuscript volumes; lecture 10.

21. Lumsden, vol. 2, lecture 40.

22. University of Edinburgh *Calendar*, 1882–83, pp. 265–66.

23. Partridge, *Landmarks*, p. 25. Partridge gives a brief review of Milton's editors, including Newton and Warton.

24. David Masson, *The Life of John Milton* (London: Macmillan, 1859–94), vol. 1, p. xi.

25. Flora Masson, "David Masson," p. 23.

Chapter 5

1. Walter William Skeat, "Introduction" to *A Student's Pastime: Articles Reprinted from Notes and Queries* (Oxford: Oxford University Press, 1896), pp. vii–viii. This sketch, eighty-four pages in length, is a surprisingly personal production for the usually self-effacing Skeat. It is not really an autobiography; Skeat explains his purpose at the outset. "A good friend of mine once asked me—'How came you to think of studying English?' The fact that such a ques-

tion was possible suggests that to do so is an uncommon course. . . . Under the circumstances, perhaps a few personal details are allowable."

2. Ibid., pp. ix–x.

3. Ibid., p. xiii.

4. Cambridge University *Calendar*, 1854–55, p. 5.

5. One exception is the Shakespearean scholar and editor Aldis Wright, son of a Baptist minister and thus quite visibly a Noncomformist. Wright studied at Trinity College, Cambridge, from 1849 until 1854; when the religious tests applying to his case were removed, he returned to Cambridge and took a B.A. in 1858. Wright remained at Cambridge until his death in 1914, serving as librarian at Trinity College and as senior bursar.

6. Skeat, A *Student's Pastime*, p. xv.

7. Ibid., p. xx.

8. Ibid., p. xxi.

9. Ibid., pp. xxv–xxvi.

10. American scholars were not left behind despite their distance from most of the sources. Child's work in Chaucer has been described. Thomas R. Lounsbury (1838–1915) made a major contribution with his three-volume *Studies in Chaucer*, 1892.

11. At the end of the "Introduction" to A *Student's Pastime*, Skeat gives a bibliography of his work to that time, consisting of fifty-nine items. The list does not seem to establish guidelines for counting up Skeat's books, however. Some revised editions are given as a note to the original entry, while others appear as separate entries. The 1886 Oxford edition of *Piers Plowman* is given as entry 43, while a total of seven previous editions of parts of the poem are given as entry 11.

12. Walter William Skeat, *The Science of Etymology* (Oxford: Oxford University Press, 1912), p. 12.

13. Skeat, "Introduction," A *Student's Pastime*, pp. lxxiv–lxxv.

14. Reprinted by the Simplified Spelling Society (London: Pitman and Sons, 1908), inside front cover. Other members of the society included Gilbert Murray and H. G. Wells.

15. Walter William Skeat, ed., *Testimonials in Favour of the Reverend Walter W. Skeat, a Candidate for the Elrington and Bosworth Professorship of Anglo-Saxon in the University of Cambridge* (Cambridge: Cambridge University Press, 1878), p. 6.

16. Ibid., p. 7.

17. Ibid., pp. 27–28; 21–22; 49.

18. Ibid., pp. 42; 25.

19. Ibid., pp. 32–33.

20. Ibid., pp. 36–37.

21. The requirements for the Medieval and Modern Languages Tripos Examination are listed in the 1890–91 Cambridge University *Calendar*, both separately and under the heading "Regulations for Various Triposes." See p. 40.

22. Cambridge University *Calendar*, 1890–91, p. 67.

23. Ibid., pp. 70–72.

24. Ibid., p. 34.

25. Potter gives a lively account of these events, *The Muse in Chains*, pp. 158–201.

26. This is the thesis of John Churton Collins's *The Study of English Literature: A Plea for Its Recognition and Organization at the Universities* (London: Macmillan, 1891). See pp. 1–6.

27. Ibid., p. 65.

28. Partridge, *Landmarks*, p. 45.

29. E. M. W. Tillyard, *The Muse Unchained: An Intimate Account of the Revolution in English Studies at Cambridge* (London: Bowes and Bowes, 1958), pp. 23–24.

30. Murray, *Caught in the Web of Words*, p. 327.

Bibliography

More complete listings of the works of Morley, Child, Masson and Skeat may be found in the *New Cambridge Bibliography of English Literature*, the *National Union Catalog*, and the *British Museum Catalogue of Printed Books*, while the *Wellesley Index to Victorian Periodicals 1824–1900* is helpful for periodical essays. The following list includes works which have been mentioned in this book or which contain background information particularly useful for the subject.

Achtert, Walter Scott. "A History of English Studies to 1883 Based on the Research of William Riley Parker." Ph.D. diss., New York University, 1972.

Adams, Eleanor Nathalie. *Old English Scholarship in England from 1500–1800*. New Haven: Yale University Press, 1917. Reprint. Hamden, Conn.: Archon Books, 1970.

Allen, Don Cameron. "The Graduate Departments of English Before 1900." In *The Ph.D. in English and American Literature: A Report to the Profession and the Public*, pp. 1–14. New York: Holt, Rinehart, Winston, 1968.

Altick, Richard D. *The English Common Reader: A Social History of the Mass Reading Public, 1800–1900*. Chicago: University of Chicago Press, 1957.

—————. *The Scholar Adventurers*. New York: Macmillan, 1950.

—————. *Victorian People and Ideas: A Companion for the Modern Reader of Victorian Literature*. New York: Norton, 1973.

Arnold, Matthew. *Higher Schools and Universities in Germany*. London: Macmillan, 1868. 2d ed., 1882.

Ayeldotte, Frank. *The Oxford Stamp, and Other Essays: Articles from the Emotional Creed of an American Oxonian*. Oxford: Oxford University Press, 1917.

Barrie, James. *An Edinburgh Eleven: Pencil Portraits of College Life*. London: Hodder and Stoughton, 1891.

Bellot, Hugh Hale. *University College, London, 1826–1926*. London: University of London Press, 1929.

Chambers, Raymond Wilson. *Concerning Certain Great Teachers of the English Language: An Inaugural Lecture Delivered in University College, London*. London: Edward Arnold, 1923.

————. *Man's Unconquerable Mind: Studies of English Writers from Bede to A. E. Housman and W. P. Kerr*. London: Jonathan Cape, 1952.

Child, Francis James, ed. *English and Scottish Ballads*. 8 vols. Boston: Little, Brown, 1857–59.

————, ed. *The English and Scottish Popular Ballads*. 10 parts in 5 vols. Boston: Houghton Mifflin, 1882–98. Reissues and reprints in varying formats. Many other editions, abridgments, etc.

————, ed. *Four Old Plays*. Cambridge, Mass.: George Nichols, 1848.

————. "Observations on the Language of Chaucer." *American Academy of Arts and Sciences* (Memoirs, 1863), New Series, 8, 445–502. Edited version, "Observations on the Language of Chaucer and Gower," in Alexander Ellis, *On Early English Pronunciation* (London: Early English Text Society, extra series, 1929; a reissue).

————. "Observations on the Language of Gower's *Confessio Amantis*." *American Academy of Arts and Sciences* (Memoirs, 1873), new series, 9, 265–315.

————, ed. *The Poetical Works of Edmund Spenser*. Boston: Houghton Mifflin, 1855.

————. *The Scholar-Friends: Letters of F. J. Child and James Russell Lowell*. Edited by M. A. Dewolfe-Howe and G. W. Cottrell, Jr. Cambridge, Mass.: Harvard University Press, 1952,

————, ed. *War-Songs for Freemen*. Boston: Ticknor and Fields, 1863.

Collins, John Churton. *The Study of English Literature: A Plea for Its Recognition and Organization at the Universities*. London: Macmillan, 1891.

Davies, the Rev. John Llewelyn, ed. *The Working Men's College 1854–1904: Records of Its History and Work for Fifty Years*. London: Macmillan, 1904.

Fallon, Daniel. *The German University: A Heroic Ideal in Conflict with the Modern World*. Boulder, Colo.: Colorado Associated University Press, 1980.

Fisher, John H. "Nationalism and the Study of Literature." *American Scholar* 49 (Winter 1979–80), pp. 105–10.

Franklin, Phyllis. "English Studies: The World of Scholarship in 1883." *PMLA* 99 (May 1984), pp. 356–70.

Furnivall, Frederick James and J. W. Hales, eds. *Bishop Percy's Folio Manuscript: Ballads and romances*. 4 vols. London: N. Trubner and Co., 1867.

Ganzel, Dewey. *Fortune and Men's Eyes: The Career of John Payne Collier*. Oxford: Oxford University Press, 1982.

Grant, Robert. "Harvard College in the Seventies." *Scribner's Magazine* 21 (May 1897), pp. 554–66.

Gross, John. *The Rise and Fall of the Man of Letters*. London: Weidenfeld and Nicolson, 1969.

Gummere, Francis B. "A Day with Professor Child." *Atlantic Monthly* 103 (March 1909), pp. 421–25.

Hart, Walter Morris. "F. J. Child and the Ballad." *PMLA* 21 (1906), pp. 755–807. Reprinted in the Dover edition (1965) of Child's *The English and Scottish Popular Ballads*.

Hustvedt, Sigurd Bernhard. *Ballad Books and Ballad Men: Raids and Rescues in Britain, America, and the Scandinavian North Since 1800*. Cambridge, Mass.: Harvard University Press, 1930.

Kittredge, George Lyman. "Francis James Child." *Atlantic Monthly* 78 (1896), pp. 737–42. In slightly altered form, this article appears in *The English and Scottish Popular Ballads*, complete editions, after 1898.

Masson, David. *The British Museum: Historical and Descriptive*. Edinburgh: R. and W. Chambers, 1858.

———. *British Novelists and Their Styles*. London: Macmillan, 1859. Lectures delivered to the Philosophical Society of Edinburgh, March and April 1858.

———. *Carlyle Personally and in His Writings*. London: Macmillan, 1885.

———. *Chatterton: A Biography*. London: Hodder and Stoughton, 1899. Rev. ed. First published in *Dublin University Magazine*, 1851. Intermediate version in *Essays Biographical and Critical*.

———. *Essays Biographical and Critical, Chiefly on the English Poets*. London: Macmillan, 1856. contents include "Shakespeare and

Goethe," "Milton's Youth," "Dryden," "Swift," "Wordsworth," "Scottish Influence on British Literature," "The Three Devils," "Theories of Poetry," "De Quincy," "Chatterton."

―――. *The Life of John Milton, Narrated in Connexion with the Poetical, Ecclesiastical, and Literary History of His Time.* 7 vols. London: Macmillan, 1859–94.

―――, ed. *Poetical Works of John Milton.* 3 vols. London: Macmillan, 1874.

―――. *Shakespeare Personally.* London: Smith, Elder and Co., 1914. Masson's University of Edinburgh lectures on Shakespeare. Edited by Flora Masson.

―――. *The Three Devils: Luther's, Milton's, and Goethe's with Other Essays.* London: Macmillan, 1874. Contents include "Shakespeare and Goethe," "Milton's Youth," "Dean Swift," "How Literature May Illustrate History."

―――. "University Teaching for Women." Edinburgh Ladies' Educational Association, *Introductory Lectures of the Second Season, 1868–69.* Edinburgh: Edmonston and Douglas, 1868.

―――. *Wordsworth, Shelley, Keats, and Other Essays.* London: Macmillan, 1874. Contents include, besides poets named in title, "Scottish Influence on British Literature," "Theories of Poetry," "Prose and Verse: De Quincey."

Masson, Flora. "David Masson." *University of Edinburgh Journal* 2 (1929–30), pp. 15–24.

Morley, Henry. *Early Papers and Some Memories.* London: G. Routledge and Sons, 1891. Contents include "How to Make Home Unhealthy" and several essays from *Household Words.*

―――. *English Writers.* 11 vols. London: Cassell and Co., 1864–95. (Vols. 1 and 2 originally published by Chapman and Hall.)

―――. *A First Sketch of English Literature.* London: Cassell and Co., 1873. Many reissues and revisions.

―――. *The Journal of a London Playgoer from 1851 to 1866.* London: G. Routledge and Sons, 1866. Theatre reviews, largely from *The Examiner.*

―――. Introductory material for several series of reprints, among them the following:

    Carisbrooke Library. 14 vols. London: G. Routledge and Sons, 1889–92.

Cassell's Library of English Literature. 5 vols. London: Cassell and Co., 1875–81.

Cassell's National Library. About 220 vols. London: Cassell and Co., 1886–91.

Morley's Universal Library. 64 vols. London: G. Routledge and Sons, 1883–88.

Murray, K. M. Elisabeth. *Caught in the Web of Words: James A. H. Murray and the Oxford English Dictionary.* New Haven: Yale University Press, 1977.

Palmer, David J. *The Rise of English Studies: An Account of the Study of English Language and Literature from Its Origins to the Making of the Oxford English School.* Oxford: Oxford University Press, 1965.

Parker, William R. "The MLA, 1883–1953." *PMLA* 68 (September 1953), part 2, pp. 3–39.

Partridge, A. C. *Landmarks in the History of English Scholarship 1500–1970.* Capetown, South Africa: Nasou Limited, 1972.

Payne, William Morton, ed. *English in American Universities by Professors in the English Departments of Twenty Representative Institutions.* Boston: Heath, 1895.

Potter, Stephen. *The Muse in Chains: A Study in Education.* London: Jonathan Cape, 1937.

Reppert, James Donald. "F. J. Child and the Ballad." Ph.D. diss., Harvard University, 1953.

Rorie, David. "The Weighty Eighties." *University of Edinburgh Journal* 6 (1933–34), pp. 8–15.

Skeat, Walter William, ed. *The Complete Works of Geoffrey Chaucer.* 7 vols. Oxford: Oxford University Press, 1894–97.

———, ed. *The Holy Gospels in Anglo-Saxon, Northumbrian, and Old Mercian Versions.* 4 parts. Cambridge: Cambridge University Press, 1871–87.

———, ed. *Lancelot of the Laik.* Early English Text Society, 1866.

———. *Notes on English Etymology, Chiefly Reprinted from the Transactions of the Philological Society.* Oxford: Oxford University Press, 1901.

———. *Questions for Examination in English Literature, Chiefly Selected from College Papers Set in Cambridge.* London: Deighton, Bell, 1873.

————. *The Science of Etymology*. Oxford: Oxford University Press, 1912.

————, ed. *Specimens of Early English*. 3 vols. With Richard Morris. Oxford: Oxford University Press, 1882.

————. *A Student's Pastime: Articles Reprinted from Notes and Queries*. Oxford: Oxford University Press, 1896.

————, ed. *Testimonials in Favour of the Reverend Walter W. Skeat, a Candidate for the Elrington and Bosworth Professorship of Anglo-Saxon in the University of Cambridge*. Cambridge: Cambridge University Press, 1878.

————, ed. *The Vision of William Concerning Piers Plowman*. 2 vols. Early English Text Society and Oxford University Press, 1867–85.

Solly, Henry Shaen. *The Life of Henry Morley, LLD*. London: Edward Arnold, 1898.

Taylor, David. *The Godless Students of Gower Street*. London: University College Union, 1968.

Tillyard, E. M. W. *The Muse Unchained: An Intimate Account of the Revolution in English Studies at Cambridge*. London: Bowes and Bowes, 1958.

Vanderbilt, Kermit. *Charles Eliot Norton: Apostle of Culture in a Democracy*. Cambridge, Mass.: Harvard University Press, 1959.

Wellek, René. *The Rise of English Literary History*. Chapel Hill: University of North Carolina Press, 1941.

Index

Dictionary of National Biography, 33, 92

Disruption (Church of Scotland), 112, 113

Dissenters. *See* Nonconformists

"Dissenting academies," 123

Divorce Tracts (Milton), 132

Dixwell, Epes Sargent, 65, 67

Doctor of Philosophy. *See* Ph.D. degree

Domesday Book, 150

Douglas, Gavin, 129

Dowden, Edward, 155

Drayton, Michael, 130

Dream of the Lilybell, The (Morley), 63

Drummond of Hawthornden, 129

Dryden, John, 54, 71, 78, 130, 161

Dublin, 155

Earle, John, 161

Early English Aliterative Poems of the West Midland Dialect of the Fourteenth Century (Morris), 20

Early English Text Society, 17–21, 52, 146–49, 164

Early Papers and Some Memories (Morley), 41, 42

East Dereham (England), 144

Edinburgh, 19; and Child, 105, 108; and Masson, 112, 113, 114, 120, 121, 133, 155

Edinburgh, University of: examinations, 128–31; Masson, 20, 40, 48, 94, 121–31; *illustration*, 97

Edinburgh Ladies' Educational Association, 134

Edinburgh Review, 47, 160

Education Act of 1870, 25

Education of Henry Adams, The (Adams), 68

Egypt, 9, 30

Elene (Cynewulf), 52

Elgin Marbles, 33

Eliot, Charles W., 23, 81

Elizabeth I (queen of England), 60

Elizabethan Society of Antiquaries, 19

Ellis, Alexander John, 101

Elrington and Bosworth Chair of Anglo-Saxon, 153–54, 157, 165

Encyclopedia Britannica, 93

English and Scottish Ballads (Child), 102, 105, 106

English and Scottish Popular Ballads, The (Child), 74, 102–8

"English and Scottish Popular Ballads, The" (seminar, Child), 109

English composition, 52–53, 122–23

English Dialect Dictionary (Wright), 99

English Dialect Society, 148

English High School (Boston), 65

English Plays (Morley), 61

"English Poets" (series), 102

English Writers (Morley), 48–49, 59, 87

"Essay on Man" (Pope), 76

Essays (Bacon), 52, 149

Essex (England), 137

Etymological Dictionary (Skeat), 164

Euripides, 70

Euston Road (London), 117

Examinations: Cambridge, 157–60; Civil Service, 161; Harvard, 91; University College, 49–52; University of Edinburgh, 128–31; University of London, 47, 49, 50

Examiner, The, 43, 45, 46

Faerie Queene, The (Spenser), 10, 51

Faucit, Helen, 46

Faulkner, William, 26

Fawkes, Guy, 36

F. J. Child and the Ballad (Reppert), 65

First Sketch of English Literature (Morley), 48, 59

First World War, 19 n. 10, 34–35

Fisher, John H., 25–26

Fletcher, Giles, 129

Folger, Henry Clay, 31

Folger Shakespeare Library, 31

ᵢᵢᵢᵢᵢ

Rawlinson Chair of Anglo-Saxon, 153, 161
Reformation, 123, 140
Regent's Park (London), 119
Regent Terrace (Edinburgh), 121
Registers of the Company of Stationers (Arber), 63
Reid, George, 96, 134
Religio Medici (Browne), 54
Reliques of Ancient English Poetry (Percy), 107
Reppert, James Donald, 65, 108
Revere, Paul, 66
Rhetoric: as academic study, 67, 94, 122–23
Richard II (Shakespeare), 149; character, 46
Richardson, Samuel, 129
Richard the Redeless (anonymous), 149
Rienzi (painting, Hunt), 119
Rise of English Studies, The (Palmer), 64
Robertson, William, 129
Robinson, Fred Norris, 109
Roman alphabet, 152
Romance and Prophecies of Thomas of Erceldoune (anonymous), 20
Romance of Alexander and Dindimus, The (anonymous), 149
Romance languages, 157
Roman literature. *See* Latin literature
Rome, 30
Romeo and Juliet (Shakespeare), 30
Rorie, David, 126
Rosalind (Shakespeare's), 27
Rosalind (Spenser's), 84
Rossetti, Christina, 118
Rossetti, Dante Gabriel, 118
Routledge, G., and Sons, 61
Roxburghe Club, 19, 70
Royal Academy (England), 45, 119
Royal Shakespeare Company, 31

Saint Andrew's Church (Edinburgh), 113
Saint Louis, University of, 22

Saint Peter, monastery of, 59
Saintsbury, George, 96, 133
Sanskrit, 14 n. 4, 50, 51
Sayer, Mary Anne, 42, 44
Schneidewinn, Friedrich Wilhelm, 73
Schoolmaster, The (Ascham), 60
Science of Etymology, The (Skeat), 150
Scotland, 3, 40, 52
Scott, Walter, 41, 121; and ballads, 108; and journals and societies, 19, 116
Seasons, The (Thomson), 10
Second World War, 38
Sedgwick, Elizabeth Ellery, 78
Seneca, 27
Shakespeare, William, 51, 54, 156, 158, 159; and Child, 78, 79, 83, 109; and Masson, 128; and Morley, 41, 60, 62; popularity of, 10, 26–31; scholars, 107; and Skeat, 138, 143; societies, 28–29; sonnets, 82
Shakespeare Personally (Masson), 128
"Shakespeare's and the Greek Tragedians' Portraits of Women" (essay topic), 76
Shakespeare's Dramatic Art (Ulrici), 128
Shakespeare Society (Philadelphia), 29
Shandon, Captain (Thackeray's), 118
Shelley, Percy, 161
Shepheardes Calendar (Spenser), 54
Shropshire (England), 42, 107, 137
Shylock (Shakespeare's), 30
Sidgwick, Henry, 156
Sidney, Philip, 47, 149
Simplified Spelling Society, 152–53
Sir Gawaine and the Green Knight (anonymous), 20
"Sir Patrick Spens" (anonymous), 103
Skeat, Walter William, 4, 35, 106, 135; achievements, 164; Cambridge, 3, 143–45, 163–66; Elring-